THE DESERT SOUTHWEST

AMERICAN DESIGN

THE DESERT SOUTHWEST

TEXT BY NORA BURBA AND PAULA PANICH
PHOTOGRAPHS BY TERRENCE MOORE
FOREWORD BY J. JACKSON WALTER,
PRESIDENT, THE NATIONAL TRUST FOR
HISTORIC PRESERVATION
INTRODUCTION BY VIRGINIA AND
LEE McALESTER
DESIGN BY JUSTINE STRASBERG

PRODUCED BY THE MILLER PRESS, INC.

BANTAM BOOKS · TORONTO · NEW YORK · LONDON · SYDNEY · AUCKLAND

THE DESERT SOUTHWEST

A Bantam Book / October 1987

Library of Congress Cataloging-in-Publication Data

Burba, Nora.
The desert Southwest.

(American design)
Bibliography: p. 245
1. Southwest, New—Description and travel—
1981- —Views. 2. Deserts—Southwest, New—
Pictorial works. 3. Southwest, New—History.
I. Panich, Paula. II. Moore, Terrence. III. Title.
IV. Series.
F787.B87   1987   979   86-47894

ISBN 0-553-05200-4

Published simultaneously in the United States and Canada

Bantam Books are published by Bantam Books, Inc. Its trademark,
consisting of the words "Bantam Books" and the portrayal of a
rooster, is Registered in U.S. Patent and Trademark Office and in
other countries. Marca Registrada. Bantam Books, Inc., 666 Fifth
Avenue, New York, New York 10103.

Printed in Italy by New InterLitho S.p.A. - Milan

0 9 8 7 6 5 4 3 2 1

ACKNOWLEDGMENTS

In putting together a book such as this, our intent was to present a variety of houses, ranging from old to new, that represented the style of the Southwest. In so doing, we received help and encouragement from countless people, many of whom became friends along the way.

First and foremost, we would like to thank the home-owners, architects, designers, and builders whose houses we have featured in this book. With patience, good humor, and enthusiasm, they allowed us into their homes and lives—often for weeks at a time. Without them, there would not have been a book.

Our deep gratitude also goes to our project editor, Jennie McGregor, whose guidance kept us on track; also to Angela Miller who found us; and all the staff of The Miller Press; and to Coleen O'Shea and Becky Cabaza of Bantam Books. Thanks also to the fine efforts of the design and production team—Tina Strasberg, Ilisha Helfman, and Pat Jerina; Ginny Croft and Grace Skelton; Ken Hurley of Adroit Graphic; and especially Nan Jernigan.

Those who helped us along the way include Kim Newton, Dan Budnik, Bill Bolinger, Carol Winner, Michael Bliss, Ann Shelton, Charles and Kay Shelton, and Barney Burns. Mahina Drees, Tom Naylor, Nancy Thibedeau, Elisa Green, Abigail Adler, and Melanie Peters are also recipients of our appreciation, as are all those too numerous to mention by name, but whose generosity and interest led, in various ways, to the final book.

Thanks to Mary and Paul Taylor, Jeffrey Cook, Stephanie Vencil, Tim and Laurie Herter, Paul Weiner, and Christine Mather. Additionally, we are indebted to Alan C. Vedder, Gary Miller of the Lincoln County Heritage Trust, John Meigs, Nora Henn, Bill Linsman, Karla Panich, and Juanita Panich.

Also our thanks go to Manya Winsted, Barbara Glynn Denney, Larry St. John, Joel and Lila Harnett, and the staff of *Phoenix Home & Garden* magazine for their support and advice. Our gratefulness is extended to Nancy Kitchell; Dirk Sutro and Gretchen Pelletier of *San Diego Home/Garden* magazine; Paul Zygas of Arizona State University's Department of Architecture; Carol Olten; Randolph Jenks; the Binns family; Wendy Black of Best Western International, and Carl Biehler. For their help with research material, we thank Laura Sammons of the Arizona Office of Tourism; the California, Texas, and New Mexico offices of tourism; the San Diego Visitors and Convention Bureau; the Arizona Historical Society; Sul Ross University; and the Museum of the Big Bend. A special thank you to Suzi Moore for her scouting and photographic talents.

Finally, we would like to dedicate this book to Suzi Moore, Juanita Panich, Ilana Panich-Linsman, and Jorgen Trulsson for their inspiration, faith, and love.

NORA BURBA,
PAULA PANICH, AND
TERRY MOORE

CONTENTS

ARIZONA 114

CALIFORNIA 200

FOREWORD

About seven miles southwest of Mountainair, New Mexico, lie the crumbling red stone walls of a seventeenth-century Franciscan mission, San Gregorio de Abo. Abo's past, in many ways, is a microcosm of New Mexico's history. It was located on a major trade route between the Great Plains and the Rio Grande and for hundreds of years was a major cultural crossroads in the desert Southwest. The site was abandoned due to crop failures and Apache attacks in the 1680s, leaving behind for today's archaeologists one of the most significant structures to survive from the Spanish frontier.

The site is significant on another count, too, in the person of its ninety-two-year-old caretaker, Federico Sisneros, the nation's oldest park ranger, whose devotion to the ruins exemplifies the relationship the people of the Southwest have with their landscape and their old buildings.

Sisneros, whose ancestors resettled the Estancia Basin area in the 1840s, has cared for the Abo, as his father did before him, since the 1890s. Curation of the site has been Sisneros's lifework. His family donated the site to the state of New Mexico in 1938, and it is now part of the Salinas National Monument. But long before governments got involved, Sisneros regularly inspected the ruins, practiced preventive maintenance of the walls and features, and made repairs. One of Sisneros's earliest recollections is his father's explanation that sheep, if not kept away from the ruins, would lick the walls to obtain extruded salt, eventually eroding the walls of the Abo.

The National Trust recognized Sisneros's devotion to the Abo in 1986 with a Preservation Honor Award for superlative achievement and leadership in historic preservation. But caring for historic sites and old buildings is not unusual in this unique part of

America. Thousands of Southwestern residents, in their own ways, are dedicated to giving superlative care to their houses, old and new.

People in the desert Southwest, and their houses, are tied deeply to a rich heritage of style and experience. By preserving this legacy, Southwesterners are contributing immensely to the vitality of their cities, towns, and rural areas. By reminding us of the accomplishments of those who came before us, this irreplaceable heritage provides a continuity and historical perspective that is of the utmost importance to the culture of our nation.

The owners of the houses in this book truly understand the spirit of stewardship, that it requires a constant investment of personal attention. Just like Federico Sisneros, they are dedicated to preserving the old and to making sure that the new is compatible with it.

J. JACKSON WALTER, PRESIDENT
NATIONAL TRUST FOR
HISTORIC PRESERVATION

THE DESERT SOUTHWEST

INTRODUCTION

The Southwestern United States, a region of scattered mountain ranges and parched deserts stretching from western Texas to California, holds a special place in the history of American dwellings. Early building traditions elsewhere in our country—the massive timber-framed or log houses of the Eastern woodlands and the sod houses of the Plains—have long been abandoned to survive principally as museum relics. In the arid Southwest, on the other hand, the traditional Spanish technique of building with bricks of sun-dried mud has continued without interruption for three centuries and is alive and well today. Over half of the remarkable houses in this collection are of adobe construction—some adapted from older structures and others newly built. All share the handmade charm and practical insulating qualities of this venerable building material.

Thick adobe walls are wonderfully permanent when protected from the desert's intermittent but torrential rains. Exterior wall surfaces were traditionally given a smooth finish coat of mud that was periodically renewed to protect the bricks beneath; on modern structures a more permanent stucco-like plaster usually serves this purpose. Roofs on traditional adobe buildings, although almost flat, were also designed to divert water from the vulnerable walls.

Massive roof-supporting logs, called vigas, were first laid atop the nearly completed walls, which were then built up a foot or two higher to extend above the finished roof as a low parapet. The roof was added in layers on top of the vigas, beginning with a series of smaller wooden crosspieces, or latillas, which were covered by a thatch-like layer of straw overlaid by a final water-resistant coating of sun-hardened mud or mortar. Care was taken to give the roof a slight pitch so that rainwater would run to one side to be passed through the wall parapet by means of spouts, or canales, that dumped it a foot or more beyond the wall.

The flat upper surfaces of the walls above the canales were particularly vulnerable to rainfall erosion and required frequent repair. A mid-nineteenth-century Anglo innovation solved this problem by capping the walls with hard kiln-fired bricks, which became a characteristic feature of Territorial adobe buildings. Still later, typical Anglo pitched roofs framed with light lumber and covered with shingles were commonly used above simple adobe walls (in rainy coastal California pitched roofs framed with heavy timbers and covered with clay tiles were traditional on Hispanic adobe houses). Some Territorial houses were further Anglicized with stylistic detailing borrowed from their wooden-framed Greek Revival (mid-nineteenth century) or Queen Anne (late nineteenth century) contemporaries.

Although most early dwellings of the arid Southwest had adobe walls, Hispanic builders were also masters of stone masonry, and a few of the most elaborate Spanish Colonial houses, as well as many mission and presidio buildings, were built of stone. Both solid stone walls and similar-appearing stone veneers over wooden framing remain favorite wall materials for contemporary Southwestern houses.

Architectural historians have always had difficulty applying neat stylistic categories to this long and evolving sequence of Southwestern building. The problem is compounded by the Historic Revival movement of the early twentieth century, which borrowed Spanish and Indian design elements and adapted them to modern houses, many of which have wooden-framed walls veneered to resemble massive adobe.

Particularly popular in the Southwest are Pueblo Revival designs that blend elements of the flat-roofed Hispanic house with details borrowed from Pueblo Indian dwellings. The pueblos have walls not of Spanish-style adobe bricks but of massive mud applied in layers, which give them a more rounded and sculpted appearance. Pueblo roofing systems, however, were similar to those used by the Spanish, except that the Indian builders, with only stone tools, were not concerned with the precise lengths of their vigas, which were left to project well beyond exterior wall surfaces. The Spanish, on the other hand, used iron saws to cut the timbers so that their ends remained unseen and protected within the adobe walls.

Indian-style projecting vigas, now sometimes used for decorative effect, are a characteristic feature of the Pueblo Revival style, which remains popular for new Southwestern dwellings. Other Historic Revival styles more closely mimic early Hispanic prototypes, and such houses are best termed Spanish Colonial Revivals to distinguish them from nineteenth-century Spanish Colonial originals. Most twentieth-century Spanish Colonial Revival houses have more elaborate details than those originally built in the remote Southwestern United States during the Spanish Colonial period. They look to the houses and churches of central Mexico, South America, and even Spain itself for their decorative precedents.

Still another stylistic problem concerns the gradually increasing Anglo influence on traditional Hispanic building practices during the last half of the nineteenth century. The Territorial style, which added only fired brick wall copings, or capstones, and modest Anglo windows and doors, is best considered a late subtype of the Spanish Colonial house, whereas adobe-walled dwellings with pitched roofs and clearcut Greek Revival or Victorian porches and decorative details are best treated as Hispanic-influenced examples of these Anglo styles.

A final trend in contemporary Southwestern design takes traditional themes—walls of sculptured stucco or stone, Hispanic interior detailing, the stepped-back profile of the pueblo—and develops them in frankly modern terms.

In the pages that follow, Nora Burba

and Paula Panich have brought together a truly exceptional collection of Southwestern houses to illustrate this long architectural heritage. Four of these—Storefront Territorial, Adobe and Stone Territorial, Victorian Adobe, and Mexican Colonial Town House—are original nineteenth-century Spanish Colonial or Hispanic-Victorian buildings adapted to modern living. Five others—Pueblo Revival, Contemporary Territorial, Contemporary Pueblo Style, Sculpted Adobe, and Spanish Colonial Revival—are twentieth-century Pueblo Revival or Spanish Colonial Revival dwellings dominated by shapes and details borrowed from the region's past. A final six—Abstracted Traditional, Rock Ranch, Prairie-Influenced Contemporary, Stone Cottage, Stone, Copper, and Glass Contemporary, and Desert Mediterranean—are modern designs based on traditional Southwestern themes. All fifteen are extraordinarily inviting houses that richly demonstrate the domestic charms of this remarkable region in both their exterior and their interior details.

One of the frustrations of most "house watching" is that it must be done from the street. The more delightful a house's exterior design and style, the greater our curiosity about what lies within. Museum houses help solve this dilemma, but only occasionally do they retain the verve and character of real-life occupants. Usually the furnishings have been brought together from many sources and reflect only a norm of the period, not the flair of a creator.

The Desert Southwest presents in permanent form a collection of houses whose interiors are a match for their exteriors—houses where creative owners have put thought into every detail, houses with furnishings that enhance their style. The houses in this book can all be enjoyed with time to relish and remember an intricate latilla pattern, the curve of a fireplace, a carved door, a window detail, or an owner's treasured collection of Southwestern art. In short, this is a book to be savored at leisure.

VIRGINIA AND LEE McALESTER,
Authors of *A Field Guide
to American Houses*

NEW MEXICO

Stories are often told about telephone operators from all over the United States getting inquiries about foreign long-distance rates to New Mexico. The post office in Albuquerque receives U.S. mail affixed with international airmail stamps. The occasional first-time visitor will bring a passport. Although it has been a part of the Union since 1912, New Mexico's 122,000 square miles can seem like a foreign country to those unfamiliar with it. More than any other state, it has held on to—and nurtured—its historic roots. Spanish flows easily from the lips of residents. Native Americans still live in ancient cities built by their forebears and participate in age-old traditions.

Yet New Mexico, which has a history and culture traceable for thousands of years, is perhaps the most "American" of all the states; it could be said that it is the cradle of this country's civilization. Long before European feet trod on Plymouth Rock, they left footprints in New Mexico.

Perhaps the first residents of New Mexico were too busy trying to survive the elements to pay much attention, but the state's spectacular geography is worthy of pause. There is a quality of light and a clarity of air that keep the scenery in brilliantly sharp focus. From the Chihuahuan and Sonoran deserts, which edge into the state in the southwest, to the Sangre de Cristo Mountains in the north, the landscape rises from low-lying zones of mesquite and cactus, through piñon and juniper regions, to high-rising forests of blue spruce and Douglas fir. Although snow caps the northern mountains in the winter and thunderstorms well up in the summer without warning, water is generally scarce in New Mexico. Since prehistoric times, civilizations have clung to the valleys along the state's rivers, most notably the Rio Grande, which virtually bisects New Mexico.

Although the presence of man in New Mexico can be traced back more than 25,000 years, it is generally thought that today's Pueblo Indians are descendants of the Anasazi, a culture that flourished from before the birth of Christ to the thirteenth century. The Anasazi, and their descendants, were mostly peaceful people, agrarian and social, who lived together in small villages.

At first their houses were only semi-permanent: pits that were dug into the ground and covered with brush. Eventually they began to build rectangular above-ground dwellings made of "puddled" mud, or mud that was applied in layers to form a wall. They made flat roofs by laying logs across the top of the walls, then crisscrossing them with thin reeds, sticks, and brush. Lacking advanced cutting tools, the Indians let the logs poke through the edges of walls. They coated the roofs with mud, building up the centers to accommodate drainage. Accumulated water could trickle through spouts in the side walls, which were built to direct the water away from the vulnerable mud walls.

Soon the mud dwellings were terraced into structures four or five stories high, with each level stepped back the depth of one unit. For defense, these pueblos (as they were later called by the Spaniards) had virtually no openings on the ground level. Ladders provided access to the upper stories.

When danger was near, the ladders were hastily pulled up.

The various Indian tribes flourished, vanished, and flourished again over the generations, but the pueblo form of housing and its culture were what the Spaniards found when they began exploring New Mexico in the sixteenth century. The first to officially inspect the state was Coronado, who came up from Mexico in 1540 through the Rio Grande valley. Searching for gold and other riches, Coronado found only mud houses and frightened, puzzled Indians.

It was not until the late sixteenth century that efforts were made to colonize New Mexico. Armed with cattle and horses (unknown beasts to the Indians), soldiers, priests, and lay people trickled into the region, determined to tame it in the name of the Spanish crown. Led by the Franciscan fathers, the Spaniards built missions and settlements. They were intent on converting the Indians, whose "pagan" ways were frowned upon, and Catholicism crept into the native culture.

In this new world, the Spaniards employed many of their building traditions and soon adapted to Indian ways as well. They taught the Indians how to make adobe bricks, mixing mud, sand, and straw, and spreading the mixture into crude forms and drying the bricks in the sun. It was a technique the Spaniards had, in turn, learned from the North Africans.

The colonizers had brought with them iron tools, most notably the ax and the adz, a cutting tool used to shape wood. The logs used for the roofs—vigas, as the Spaniards called them—could now be made into square shapes; corbels and other forms of wooden trim were possible. The Spaniards quickly adapted to the concept of the enjarradora, or woman plasterer. While the Pueblo men learned adobe making, wood working, and other skills, they considered it to be woman's work to coat a building's walls with a mud plaster, giving the adobe a soft, sculpted quality.

Both in the secular and missionary settlements, the colonists' buildings were faced inward around a central plaza, which served as both the heart of the village and as a protective zone against attacks. When danger threatened, livestock and residents gathered in the plaza, and the gates were quickly shut. On the inside, portals, or covered walkways, offered protection from the brutal sun.

Furniture made during this period of Spanish colonization was simple and solid, made of whatever local wood could be found. Often decorated with carvings, many of the better pieces were made for the church, since private dwellings were sparsely furnished. Although the typical Spanish colonial residence often lacked basics such as tables, chairs, or beds, it had some chests for storage and a trastero, or a free-standing cupboard, for dishes or books. Today these pieces are popular in antiques markets.

By the early nineteenth century, the Spaniards had lost their hold in the New World. Mexico gained independence in 1821, and New Mexico became part of its lands. With independence, Mexico opened up trade with the United States. Once the Santa Fe Trail linked New Mexico to Missouri, more sophisticated building materials filtered into the state. From the south, trade with Mexico was steady as well.

In 1846 the United States moved in on New Mexico, claiming it as a territory soon after that. Military outposts were established to protect inhabitants from attack by hostile Indians and, later, to defend the territory against the Confederate Army during the Civil War. Mining and ranching concerns sprouted throughout the state, and frontier violence was a fact of life in some areas, as differing factions tried to gain control.

Architecture, during those days, began to take on a veneer of civilization, as trade brought in glass, iron, tin, and more building tools. The rounded, earthy forms of adobe began to change into buildings sporting crisper corners and brick-edged parapets. Slender columns graced doorways, and window frames often were capped with pediments.

By the late nineteenth century, the railroad linked New Mexico with the rest of the country, and Eastern styles flooded the state. Venerable adobes, including the Palace of the Governors in Santa Fe, a public building dating to the 1600s, were given the "fashionable" treatment as Victoriana swept the

state. Along the railroads, a picture book of many styles could be seen: Queen Anne, Greek Revival, Romanesque Revival, even Prairie School. All had their merits, but the Spanish-Indian influences were in imminent danger of melting back into the earth.

Not long after New Mexico became a state, concern began to arise regarding the loss of indigenous architecture and art. That, coupled with the notion of bringing tourism—that is, economic survival—to the cities of Taos and Santa Fe, prompted the birth of the Pueblo Revival style of architecture characterized by rounded adobe walls, flat roofs, and protruding vigas, or beams. In 1916 the Fine Arts Museum of Santa Fe was built in this new mode of design, and town leaders spurred the passage of stricter building codes to protect indigenous architectural structures. The Palace of the Governors, located on Santa Fe's main plaza, was stripped of its modern-day "improvements." With that, the look of Taos and Santa Fe developed.

As this was happening, the allure of Santa Fe and Taos, in particular, began to draw artists, writers, and intelligentsia from the East and Europe. Indian and Hispanic artists began to be recognized. The Rio Grande and Taos schools of art developed, and the noted Los Cinco Pintores (The Five Painters) was formed in Santa Fe. Georgia O'Keeffe, Laura Gilpin, Edward Hopper, Paul Strand, Alexander Hogue, Ansel Adams, and others let the clear New Mexico light refresh their work. As these artists moved to New Mexico, they embraced the local building styles, often handcrafting their own unique adobes, stretching the mud with their artistic sensibilities.

Today New Mexico is still a developing state. Artists and those seeking alternative lifestyles are drawn to the mountains and high deserts. Building with adobe is very much alive and well, going hand-in-hand with a popular interest in solar technology and energy conservation. Although there is a definite romance with the past, the future is accepted as well. As it was a home to new ideas earlier this century, New Mexico embraces the experimental, the untried. It is still a wide-open territory.

PUEBLO REVIVAL

A FAMILY COMPOUND IN THE SANTA FE RIVER CANYON

Shadows fall over an entrance to the house (LEFT), which leads to the kitchen. Hanging ristras, or strings of chiles, a hallmark of the Santa Fe decorative style, and woven straw form a delicate composition next to a New Mexican bench, which dates from the 1930s.

Horses have been on the property since the late 1920s (RIGHT). The owner believes the Spanish made a grievous error in abandoning their own tradition of pitched roofs for the Pueblo Indians' leaky flat ones. He has had to reroof the stable, as well as many other buildings in the compound, several times.

The setting of northern New Mexico is one where mountains rise above desert, plain, and mesa. The weather here can change quickly and dramatically. Thundering summer showers last only minutes; wind and snow blow bitterly cold in winter, but fine, unfiltered sunlight shows itself at some point almost every day of the year.

New Mexico can feel like a foreign country to those unfamiliar with its ways. Its countryside and cityscapes are dotted with traditional adobe structures, both old and new, which are reminders of a rich, long history steeped in Indian, Spanish, and Anglo-American cultures.

The architecture of northern New Mexico, sometimes called Santa Fe style, draws its distinctive character from Hispanic as well as Indian influences. The first rectangular, stepped-back pueblos were built of mud by prehistoric Indians. The Spanish introduced the use of adobe bricks and stylistic modifications such as portals and enclosed patios. The simple, dramatic sculptural shapes of the Spanish missions with their arches and bell towers met with the broken silhouettes of the pueblos to create a new style that was to

remain firmly a part of the architectural vernacular of the Southwest.

Toward the middle of the nineteenth century, the arrival of large numbers of Anglo-Americans into the Territory of New Mexico had a marked impact economically and culturally on the indigenous Hispanics and Native Americans. When the Santa Fe Trail, which stretched 800 miles from Independence, Missouri, to Santa Fe, became somewhat safe from Indian attacks, new building materials and architectural ideas followed the trail to Santa Fe. Millwork and brick, double-hung windows, and Victorian bric-a-brac made their way to the territory, and soon Santa Fe's adobe structures were trimmed with wood around windows and doorways, wainscoting appeared on interior walls, and buildings were capped with brick cornices and washed with lime stucco.

These adaptations, however, caused civic and cultural leaders in Santa Fe to fear for their community's architectural heritage. They urged builders to abandon turn-of-the-century details and return to the adobe style of their cultural roots.

As a result, in 1909–1913, the Palace of the Governors was restored to its original pueblo style. This historic government building, which dominates Santa Fe's central plaza, had acquired Victorian embellishments such as a balustrade running the length of its parapet wall. Once the ornate bric-a-brac was removed, the building looked almost as it had in the seventeenth century, with a simple portal of thick, rounded posts and protruding vigas, or beams. When the architects I.H. and W.M. Rapp designed New Mexico's building for the 1915 Panama-California Exhibition in San Diego, they created one of the first Pueblo Revival buildings. The structure, which still stands in Balboa Park, represented a rebirth of traditional New Mexican architectural forms.

16

A circular drive winds by the Pueblo Revival house (FAR LEFT). To the right is the kitchen entrance; beyond lie an adobe garage and other outbuildings.

A screen door carved by José Dolores López (1868–1937) (MIDDLE LEFT). López's delightful carved trees, angels, and small animals made his doors extremely popular; by the end of the 1920s, owning one was a necessity among aficionados of the Santa Fe style. His initials (BOTTOM LEFT), whether penciled or carved, as in this door, were essential to the successful marketing of his work.

Several generations of builders have left their mark on the house (TOP LEFT). Windows are "footed" underneath, a form of buttressing that strengthens the wall base. Protruding vigas along the wall are typical of its Pueblo Revival style, as are the vertical pilasters on the second story which cast strong shadows with pattern and depth.

Santa Fe was fast sliding into an economic decline around the turn of the twentieth century. The closest railroad stop was still fifteen inconvenient miles outside Santa Fe, so its trains were bringing far fewer tourists than local residents hoped for. Leaders of the newly organized art museum decided to take on the task of attracting tourists to their town; they were certain it was the traditional adobe style that would interest those seeking a taste of the old Southwest.

The Fine Arts Museum was built in 1916 in the new adobe style, and even before the building was finished, a local architectural competition was organized to encourage architects and artists to design in the Pueblo Revival style. The look was based on the traditional Indian pueblos and on the Spanish mission churches. Especially influential were the convent and church of Acoma, a Catholic mission built at Acoma Pueblo in the seventeenth century, whose design was the inspiration for the Panama-California Exhibition building and the Fine Arts Museum.

While the new style flourished, Santa Fe was beginning to follow Taos as a colony for artists. Well-known painters such as George Bellows and Robert Henri moved to Santa Fe in the late 1910s. They were followed by many others who were likewise attracted to the rare beauty of the centuries-old town perched 7,000 feet above sea level.

In the 1920s, painter John Sloan moved to Santa Fe and banded together with others to form *Los Cinco Pintores* (the Five Painters). Building adobe houses and studios, they began a colony of artists and writers on Camino del Monte Sol. Later another group came to form the Rio Grande Painters, and among them was E. Boyd, who was to become the undisputed expert on local Hispanic arts and crafts for her time.

Into this atmosphere came the Field family, a Philadel-

phia couple and their daughter, then in her twenties. A family diary recorded the daughter's first impressions of Santa Fe; she was appalled at what an awful, dirty place it seemed to be, with deplorable mud houses devoid of color. It was an ironic observation, as the Fields later became stalwart defenders of the Santa Fe style and their descendants still own a remarkable Pueblo Revival adobe home in the Santa Fe River Canyon.

The Fields bought a small 1870s adobe farmhouse from a local Spanish family in the mid-1920s. In 1928–29, the farmhouse was expanded and restored in the Pueblo Revival style, growing to accommodate two families of different generations. The additions were of adobe brick construction, with rough surfaces, rounded corners, massive walls, rough window lintels, a flat roof with rough-hewn, protruding vigas—all elements of the style. The house's second story is stepped back, which is also typical.

A gracious living room, sitting rooms, and three bedrooms were added to the downstairs, and second-story bedrooms were added to the house in the late 1930s. Second stories are unusual in adobe houses because of the difficulty in building adobe walls thick enough to sustain the weight of a second floor. The problem was solved with a steel beam hidden in the carved Spanish Colonial beams in the living room ceiling.

The ceilings in the house represent almost every viga and latilla, or roof decking, variation known to Santa Fe. Some rooms have herringbone-designed or split-cedar latillas, and some have no latillas at all but beams or round vigas set into coved or flat plaster. In a short passageway from the main living room into a small front room there are hand-painted latillas in many colors, an unusual interpretation of the tradition.

The central fireplace in the house is well-known among aficionados of the Santa Fe style. Artist and woodcarver Celso Gallegos of Agua Fria, New Mexico, told the family he wanted to make "one last fireplace" like those he remembered in the old Spanish ranches of the 1880s. Gallegos was one of the first woodcarvers to renew the art of carving religious images during the revival of Spanish Colonial arts and crafts around Santa Fe in the 1920s. He told the family that if they did not like his work, he would rip out the fireplace and begin anew. They loved it. It is called a shepherd's fireplace because of its banco, or built-in seating area, and its overhang, both places where people could sleep warmly on cold northern New Mexico nights. An exact copy of this fireplace is in the Smithsonian Institute in Washington, D.C.

The house grew proudly, without benefit of an architect. At first, the present owner's grandfather, who was an excellent woodworker, planned the expansions. Later, the 1930s, his daughter, Lois Field, served as her own architect and interior designer in the best New Mexican tradition, threatening once to stop speaking to a friend when he considered hiring an architect to expand his own adobe home.

The originial two-and-a-half-acre farm in the high desert flourished with apricot, cherry, peach, quince, and apple trees because of its proximity to the river and the elaborate acequia, or irrigation system. The Indians of New Mexico have practiced irrigation since prehistoric times, when they first diverted water from streams into fields. The acequia system in Santa Fe, however, was set up by the Spanish, who had learned it from the Moors. The system was labor intensive because the delivery of water had to be precisely timed. Bill Field, the present owner, remembers sailing toy boats in the water of the acequias as a young boy, and recalls that cleaning out the system was an annual three-day affair requiring the effort of almost every man in town.

Santa Fe, and New Mexico in general, lost a great number of men in World War II. Without manpower, the acequia system died, too, and well-irrigated farmland in the Santa Fe Canyon reverted to desert. The quince trees survived and continue to bear fruit on the property, testimony to their suitability to the climate.

The war had other effects on the Santa Fe Canyon. When Lois Field took her place as mistress of the house, she was a well-known hostess and patron of the arts in Santa Fe. Almost daily at five o'clock, a coterie from the bohemian art community arrived for cocktails at the Pueblo Revival house and

Light floods through a deeply recessed window, illuminating a collection of retablos, or religious paintings on flat boards. The retablos have been gathered from New Mexico, Greece, Mexico, and Puerto Rico; the one on the top far left belonged to the owner's grandfather. Handwoven blankets are cleverly displayed from a dowel suspended from the ceiling. The blanket on the top left was woven by the Rio Grande Spanish and was used as a jerga, a heavyweight woven wall or floor covering. A Peruvian blanket is in the center, next to one woven in India. The bottom blanket was woven during the 1930s, when the centuries-old Spanish Rio Grande blanket-weaving tradition was revived through the efforts of the Works Progress Administration. This is an example of a five-star Vallero blanket. Hanging also from the dowel are silver spurs from Peru, a traditional Navajo Indian bridle, and a Navajo medicine man's pouch. The two well-weathered traditional New Mexican chairs were purchased at the annual Santa Fe Spanish market held every summer in July. The chairs, of undetermined age, derive from the French style that was popular in Mexico in the eighteenth century.

22

were greeted by Oscar, the white-jacketed butler, at the door. Drinks were served by a uniformed maid until seven, when dinner, prepared by the cook, was served. After the war the elegant way of life changed. Although entertaining continued in the Santa Fe Canyon, it was never as elaborate or as frequent.

In 1938, however, the house boasted Santa Fe's second swimming pool. It was excavated by a man with a wheelbarrow harnessed to a donkey. The pool was filled with icy well water, but even during Santa Fe's short warm period, it was cold and difficult to maintain. Later the pool was filled with

dirt, but the lovely hand-made tiles with aquatic designs have survived and remain in view as rather exotic relics of a former time.

In the late 1940s, an exterior porch was enclosed to become a solarium. Four guest houses were added to the north portion of the property, along with a double garage, horse stable, laundry, tack room, and other structures. A friend recalls seeing Lois Field, one afternoon in the late 1940s, who was then well into mid-life, wielding an ax, ripping out the work done by a hard-working carpenter who had been toiling on the guest apartments. "I just hate these

One of the solarium's interior doors faces into the dining room. Supporting posts, carved corbels, and the supporting lintel remain from an original exterior patio. The twelve straw-inlay crosses, bought at Santa Fe's Spanish market, were made by children. The craft is an ancient one, possibly inherited by the Spanish from the Moors. The Franciscan monks and friars who came to New Mexico in the seventeenth century were not able to bring religious art with them, so local folk art had to take the place of elaborate gold and mother-of-pearl work. The craft was revived in the 1930s. A small bulto of the Virgin rests in a modern tin niche above the door. Through the door is the dining room table, a 1915 wedding gift to the owner's mother. On the right side of the dining room is a cleverly encased and concealed radiator installed in the 1920s.

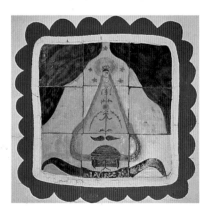

Silver spurs from Peru, once belonging to the owner's mother, hang from a living room viga (TOP LEFT).

This niche (UPPER MIDDLE LEFT) has been carved into plaster for displaying art objects. Within it sits a typical Pueblo Revival chest with a latilla-ribbed inset door and an example of a Hopi Indian kachina doll. In the Hopi religion, more than three hundred kachinas, or gods, representing different forms of life, reside in the San Francisco peaks in northern Arizona. The kachina cult, with its depiction of gods in masks and costumes, developed around A.D. 1350. This particular kachina is a symbol of the Salako mana —Salako spirits bring health and prosperity.

The group of tiles (LOWER MIDDLE LEFT) under an exterior portal were made by the owner's mother and compose a portrait of Our Lady of Guadalupe, an important Southwestern representation of the Virgin.

Ornamental tinwork such as that found on this pierced tin light-switch plate (LOWER LEFT) has been made in the Southwest since the 1800s, when tin was first imported from Mexico. After 1846 the United States Army brought in tin, which New Mexican craftsmen shaped into picture frames, chandeliers, niches, and other decorative or religious items.

The front room (RIGHT) was one of the last to be added during the late 1920s renovation. The bench and tables are twentieth century in origin and are typically New Mexican in style; the blanket on the bench is an example of Rio Grande weaving. The soft doeskin boots originated with a Plains Indian tribe, and the bells draped across the fireplace are old sleigh bells from New England. The elaborate carved niche to the left of the fireplace is from the Spanish Colonial period. The largest crucifix has been of some amusement to the family. Spanish Colonial scholar E. Boyd found it unusual as well: it is a depiction of San Juan in a Mexican military uniform.

A cobalt blue table umbrella and lounge chair on the flagstone patio sparkle in Santa Fe's summer sun. Spoke-patterned iron chairs show Art Deco influence and date from the 1920s. Beyond lie the horse stables and the garden.

In the solarium (RIGHT), large windows and two skylights let in the sunlight; shutters open to a next-door bedroom admit light there as well. The roof is a combination of peeled cedar vigas and tongue-in-groove wood paneling; the flagstone floor is covered with a contemporary sisal rug.

straight lines," she insisted as she chopped away, being devoted as she was to the curved shapes of the Pueblo style.

Bill and Maureen Field and their five children moved from the East Coast into the house in 1976. Except for a major kitchen renovation, most of their changes have been cosmetic. They modernized the kitchen, removing the special sinks that were used exclusively for china and crystal and for pots and pans and installing modern appliances. They retained the spacious dark wood cabinets and increased the counter space, which they covered in brilliant cobalt-blue tile. The remodeled kitchen is the heart of the house. It is a spacious,

cheerful, high-ceilinged room where the family can eat informally at a round table. There is a great deal of workspace and places to stash treasures the children have made at school. Its bright, cheerful tile is set off by collections of dried flowers, local pottery, and whimsical folk art pieces.

Elsewhere in the house, the Fields removed heavy Victorian furniture, Chinese lacquered tables and screens, and a grand piano topped with a fringed scarf. They kept art objects and simple Southwestern furniture, such as a pair of New Mexican chairs. The younger Fields felt the house had a museum-like atmosphere, and when they brought in their

A typical structural element of the Pueblo Revival adobe house includes this decorative, carved lintel.

Adobe naturally reflects light. Here, sunlight dapples the soft, rounded shapes of the buttressed wall and its deep windows (LEFT).

own possessions, they were pleased with the results. Many of the couches and chairs brought from the East are contemporary and neutral, and the eclectic mix works well within the classic adobe walls.

The interior spaces of the house are dominated by collections gathered over two generations. Beautiful examples of Hispanic crafts abound, including Rio Grande weaving, straw inlaid crosses, ornate tinwork, and carved and painted images of the saints. In almost every room, books fill shelves and are stacked on tables and desks. The objects and books clearly reflect a family with wide-ranging cultural interests.

Among the folk and fine art, books and plants, is a mixture of contemporary, antique, and eighteenth- and nineteenth-century New Mexican furniture. In the dining room, table and chairs from turn-of-the-century Philadelphia are used often by the family, and a matching buffet displays sterling silver serving sets that have been collected over the generations.

The house is a wonderful spot for children, with countless hiding places. For sixty years, the property has been a family compound. Rooms await the older children for their frequent visits home, and the house once again serves as a gathering place for an extended family.

STOREFRONT TERRITORIAL

HISTORY AND PAGEANTRY ON THE SQUARE IN OLD MESILLA

Morning illuminates the Mesilla plaza (LEFT). The main entrance to the Taylor residence is two doors to the left of the Del Sol sign. The plaza shows typical characteristics of the Territorial adobe style, with its straight, simple lines, wood trim, and brickwork capping the peaked rooflines of the buildings.

A painted bulto, or figure in the round, of Our Lady of Guadalupe, a saint who appeared before a Mexican peasant in the sixteenth century, stands in a niche in the adobe wall on the back of the property (RIGHT). The wall, which collapsed a few years ago and was rebuilt, dates from the 1850s.

The jagged Organ Mountains overlooking the Mesilla Valley of southern New Mexico cradle people who trace their ancestry to the Native Americans of the region, Mexicans from the state of Chihuahua, mid-nineteenth-century Spaniards from northern New Mexico, and Anglo-Americans who made the trip to the frontier from the eastern seaboard in the late 1850s.

In the town of Mesilla, just north of El Paso, Texas, one Spanish descendant has traced his ancestry to a soldier who marched bravely into New Mexico with Coronado in 1540. He is J. Paul Taylor, teacher and historian, who along with his historian wife, Mary, live in a rambling, one-story New Mexico Territorial-style adobe house on the west side of Mesilla's historic town plaza.

The town of Mesilla, which literally means "little table land," sits on a mesa near the Rio Grande. It was originally colonized by Mexican families who came to the area with Father Ramon Ortiz. The priest was commissioned by the Mexican government to bring its citizens back into Mexican domain from territory ceded to the United States in the 1848

An early-nineteenth-century New Mexican santos of Santiago, or St. James the Apostle (ABOVE LEFT). In Spanish religious lore, he arrived to help the Christians drive out the Moors.

These manos and metates, stones used by Southwestern Indians for grinding corn, were collected from Indian campgrounds and date from the prehistoric period in New Mexico (ABOVE RIGHT).

A small, sunny patio (RIGHT) lies between the house's entrance and its rear living quarters. At the far end, an exterior portal protects artifacts collected from around Mesilla. The old cooking utensils, lanterns, and an old Spanish fanega, an instrument used to measure grain, are set off by the stark white trim of the Territorial-style double-hung window (FAR RIGHT).

Treaty of Guadalupe Hidalgo, which marked the end of the Mexican War.

Enclosing themselves around a town square or plaza for better defense against marauding Apaches, the pioneering Mexican families used jacales, or mud-chinked poles and branches, as the basis of the first dwellings; permanent adobe structures came later, including the one that now belongs to the Taylors. According to the earliest record, title to the house, which forms the south portion of the Taylor property, was held in 1854 by a pioneering settler.

The Gadsden Purchase in 1853 made the community part of the United States. By 1858 settlers from the East were arriving on the Butterfield stagecoach, and Mesilla became an amalgam of Mexican, Spanish, and Anglo-American cultures. The prospering community became the political center for southern New Mexico and Arizona and an important commercial link to west Texas, northern New Mexico, and Sonora and Chihuahua in Mexico. For the thirty-year period after the Gadsden Purchase, the town was the seat of county government and the principal distribution center for the area's mining camps and military settlements.

Mesilla was at one time the largest town between San Diego, California, and San Antonio, Texas. A century ago,

however, commerce and government abandoned it in favor of Las Cruces, where the railroad made its southern New Mexico stop. Today Mesilla is one of the Southwest's best-known historic communities.

The façade of Taylor house is an example of Territorial style at its most refined. The house was once a simple, rectangular adobe. Around the turn of the century, it was modified in keeping with the style of Victorian architecture popular at the time. The windows were enlarged and trimmed with wood; a parapet was added, as were transoms above the windows and doors. The materials for these changes and trimmings were brought to the Territory of New Mexico with the coming of the railroad.

From its earliest days, the Taylor property had two shops facing the Mesilla plaza and was separated by a covered zaguán, or passageway, leading to living quarters in the rear. By 1857 the title to the major portion of the property was held by Mariano Yrissari, a well-known trader and sheep rancher from a small community near Albuquerque. In 1861 Yrissari sold out to Maria Rafaela Garcia Barela, wife of another merchandising entrepreneur, who continued to own it until 1903 and whose son maintained a store on the property.

The American Civil War brought unrest and confusion to Mesilla. The town of 2,500 became the capital of the Con-

The oratorio, or small chapel (LEFT), was added in 1972. The fan window was salvaged from the original Catholic Church in Mesilla. The gold-embroidered vestments in front of the altar belonged to Father Jean Grange, a previous resident of the house. The eighteenth-century Mexican Colonial bench was purchased from a Socorro, Texas, antiques dealer. The white altar cloth was given to Paul Taylor by the Sisters of the Good Shepherd, a local convent, and on the altar are bread flowers made for Corpus Christi Day and an Italian chalice. The New Mexican Cristos is from the eighteenth century.

This carved bulto (ABOVE) was crafted by a contemporary wood-carver from Cordova, New Mexico, George Lopez. The figure is known as San Ysidro Labrador, or St. Isadore the Laborer, the patron saint of farmers. By his side is the angel Gabriel, who has come to drive his oxen while he prays.

federate Territory of Arizona until 1862, when a significant Union victory at Glorieta Pass near Santa Fe destroyed Confederate supply lines. The Confederates left New Mexico, but wounds from the divisions caused by the war would reopen periodically during heated election campaigns, such as the campaign of 1871, when a bloody riot left nine citizens dead.

Among those who died in the violence was a much-beloved man in the community, John Lemon, whose restored tombstone can be found in the zaguán leading from the plaza to the Taylor living quarters. The Taylors rescued pieces of the tombstone in 1976, when extensive restoration was done on the brick-paved plaza. Mary Taylor surmises that when the town's original adobe church on the plaza's north side was replaced by the existing Romanesque-style Church of San Albino in 1906, Lemon's tombstone, along with that of his daughter who died of typhoid in the 1860s, was plowed under.

The restored tombstones are not the Taylor residence's only link to the Church of San Albino.

William Charles Reynolds acquired the Barela property around the turn of the century. In 1903–1904 he unified the property and refurbished it in the Territorial style of the time. In addition to enlarging the windows and adding transoms, he added a long gallery that leads from the house's entrance along the living room, dining room, and music room. The house was opened up by removing doorways to make a complete unit.

In 1917 Father Jean Grange foreclosed on a mortgage on the complex, and the property passed from the Reynolds family to the parish priest of San Albino. Father Grange used the living quarters as a rectory and taught catechism to Mesilla's young people in the Barela store. When he died in 1937, the property passed to his housekeeper, Perla Alidib. In 1953 Mary and Paul Taylor bought a portion of the house from her. In time, they would buy the entire property from the former housekeeper and would own one-half of the plaza, as they do today.

"Don't ask me the square footage, please," begs Paul Taylor. The meandering house seems to hold surprises at every turn. On an unguided tour through the house and its treasures, it is best to note a landmark to find the way back to the entrance.

When the Taylors bought the first portion of the property from Mrs. Alidib in 1953, serious restoration ensued to make the house habitable for their growing family. Mrs. Alidib had divided the house into small rental units and the Taylors required a unified house. Rooms were restored to their original purposes. A rotted wooden floor in the kitchen was replaced with tile; the dirt floor of the zaguán leading from the dining room to the bedrooms was covered for the first time; and because few rooms had electricity, the house was completely rewired. Indoor plumbing did not exist anywhere within the house, so two bathrooms were added.

In several rooms, the ceiling latillas had rotted away; where they were impossible to replace, the Taylors plastered between the vigas. Because fireplaces were the only source of heat, the Taylors added central heating for the family's comfort. The process of conservation and preservation has been slow, and the Taylors feel more needs to be done.

The initial zaguán, which holds the Lemons' grave markers, opens onto a small, sunny patio planted with potted geraniums, petunias, marigolds, and small desert shrubs. A few treasures are collected here under the portal: an old wagon seat, an antique wine press, a leathermaker's repair stool, and two trunks, one once belonging to a soldier at Fort Fillmore, which operated nearby from 1849 until 1861.

Stepping inside the next zaguán, it is clear the interior space is very special. The Taylors are collectors of art, ranging from a collection of Indian pottery and eighteenth-century Cristos, or Christ figures, and santos, or figures of saints, to the paintings of Dorthea Weiss, a Yale University-trained painter who lived most of her life in the Mesilla Valley. Every corner, niche and square foot of wall space has its own piece of eighteenth-, nineteenth-, or twentieth-century art, most of it steeped in the rich history of northern Mexico and New Mexico. There are also antique Spanish pieces, a late-eighteenth-century Philadelphia Chippendale chest, and a nineteenth-

The living room, part of the 1972 addition to the house, is filled with New Mexican folk art collections. Sunlight streams through gothic leaded-glass windows onto a tan and pale blue dhurrie rug. Both the windows and the vigas and latillas used on the ceiling are architectural remnants, salvaged from the demolition of a protestant church in El Paso and nearby adobe buildings. The portraits above the couch are of the owner's great-grandparents.

A special corner (FAR LEFT) in the living room is devoted to New Mexican art. The chair and chest are fine examples of eighteenth-century New Mexican furniture making. The tall robed figure in the corner is of Jesus Nazareno (Jesus of Nazarene). This particular bulto is carried each year in the Good Friday procession on the Mesilla plaza. Placed on top of the chest is a bulto of Nuestra Senora (Our Lady), and on the wall above is a retablo, or painted figure, of Gerturdis (St. Gertrude). All are important pieces of Spanish Colonial art in New Mexico.

The eighteenth-century Mexican baroque painting of Jesus Nazareno, was once part of a church altarpiece. It now hangs in a place of honor in the music room (LEFT), which contains a twentieth-century German Zimmermann piano. The book of music was bound in the late nineteenth century by Paul Taylor's grandfather for his mother, who played beautifully and collected sheet music. The book is half in Spanish, half in English.

A late-eighteenth-century trastero, or cupboard (ABOVE), is one of the Taylor's prized New Mexican antiques. Next to the trastero is a baker's paddle and on top, next to an Indian pot, sits a carved bulto of San Antonio, or Saint Anthony, by George Lopez.

39

A collection of nineteenth- and twentieth-century New Mexican tin frames and niches are beautifully displayed against white plastered walls. Tinwork is a highly developed and prized folk art in New Mexico.

century rope-spring bed from Virginia. The gallery, added in the 1904 restoration, is used as exhibition space for Mary Taylor's photography.

The eclecticism of the assembled art, furniture, and textiles works well in this Territorial house. The white adobe walls seem to graciously absorb all centuries and cultures. In addition, there is a serenity and spiritual depth in the home that seem to match the solidity of the thick adobe walls; the house can seem to be a sanctuary, despite its obvious family activity.

The dining room, which the Taylors feel is the heart of their home, opens onto the first interior zaguán. Among its treasures is a Gothic niche carved by Father Jean Grange, which holds a nineteenth-century Mexican santo. The long dining room table, which seats sixteen, is prized by the family.

Also found along the north wall and overlooking the patio are a guest bedroom, a music room with a fine eighteenth-century German piano, and a parlor that is presided over by two enormous paintings of Paul Taylor's Spanish great grandparents. They were the grandparents of his mother, Doña Margarita, a grand lady who was a descendant of the great dons of New Mexico. Her father was a delegate to the United States Congress from New Mexico.

South of the dining room along a second passageway is a cluster of four bedrooms, two of which, along with a small studio apartment, are the only remaining rooms that were part of the original property. The rooms still have their original ceilings, in which cottonwood vigas under latillas made from small saplings are covered by a layer of reeds called tules and then by an earthen roof.

Behind the kitchen is a bedroom-study, and beyond it is the original wine room, now used by Mary Taylor for storage of materials related to her project of eighteen years, a history of the Mesilla Valley. The room is still pungent with the smell of sour wine; when the Taylors bought the house, its previous owner told them many stories about how local Indians hired by the parish priest worked the grapes with bare feet in the room.

In 1972 an L-shaped section of the old barnyard was enclosed to make a lovely large living room and an exquisite small chapel called an oratorio. Paul Taylor refers to this addition as the "inner L." The east wall of the living room follows along the outer division of what was once the old portal, or porch, which ran along the yard. The vigas and latillas used on the ceiling of the new rooms were salvaged from part of

A charming painted niche is located in an interior passageway (ABOVE). The painting of the Holy Spirit descending was brushed more than thirty years ago. The nativity scene is composed of contemporary kiln-fired clay pieces by the Aguilar sisters of Ocotlán, Mexico. The dried sotol, or desert spoon (actually juniper and pieces of yucca), was saved from a Palm Sunday procession around the Mesilla plaza.

A late-eighteenth-century Mexican Cristos hangs in an entryway (LEFT). It is lit by natural light and by candles in tin sconces from Mesilla's original church. The Cristos, made of pine, is from a village near the Mexican city of Chihuahua.

the servants' quarters and from the storage area of the historic Nestor Armijo house in nearby Las Cruces.

To the west of the wine room is the old barn, restored and now rented to a local artist. The old carriage house in the northwestern corner of the house is in the process of restoration. The Taylors have stabilized its worn adobe walls and kept the structure's original vigas.

Fortunately, the Taylor house, which is on the National Register of Historic Places, will be preserved by their children as a New Mexico cultural resource. One son, an archeologist, is using videotape to catalog his parents' historical and contemporary collections. The work of one generation will be passed on to the next, and the house will persist as a vital witness to a piece of New Mexico history.

ADOBE AND STONE TERRITORIAL

THE NINETEENTH CENTURY PRESERVED IN LINCOLN COUNTY

Gnarled cottonwoods (LEFT) thrive along an irrigation ditch filled with water diverted from the Hondo River. The old batten-and-board ranch building with its sagging corregated-tin roof was probably used for storage in the late 1800s. It is located on the ranch road near the main house.

The three-sectioned white door (RIGHT) with its multiple-paned surround is a modern adaptation of doors frequently found on Territorial houses in New Mexico. Through the entry can be seen another door with colored leaded glass from San Francisco. This leads to the north portal. The bleached steer skull to the right is a common symbol of the Southwest.

Cattle ranches dot New Mexico's Lincoln County, where apple orchards flourish and geese and mallards fly through tall alleys of native cottonwood trees. A mild climate and rolling hills green with mesquite make this an idyllic, almost magical place.

It was not always so. In 1869 Lincoln County comprised one-quarter of the Territory of New Mexico and its population included the Mescalero Apaches. The frontier post of Fort Stanton was established here in 1855, and after the American Civil War, Hispanics from Mexico began settling in the fertile valleys of the Bonito, Hondo, and Ruidoso rivers. The history of the region is steeped in frontier bloodshed, and controversy still smolders over what triggers were pulled with whose compliance in an infamous bout of violence known as the Lincoln County War.

In 1869, the largest of Las Placitas del Rio Bonito, the villages on the Bonito River, was chosen as the county seat because of its proximity to Fort Stanton. Its name was soon changed to Lincoln, and the Mexican-style village, with less than fifteen adobe homes and fewer than 400 residents, be-

The two-story adobe section of the house is framed by cottonwoods. The simple, straightforward design of the house is graced by portals on its north and south sides. The pitched roof and two-story construction are characteristic of the utilitarian style brought to the West by the United States Army in the late 1800s. Two-storied adobe structures are unusual because adobe is structurally solid only up to about ten feet without internal supports. In this case, the wall was built with a broad base to support its weight.

Red hollyhocks tower behind the black wrought-iron Victorian-style fence that runs along one side of the house (RIGHT). The fence was brought from the East to New Mexico by railroad in the 1880s; at that time very little iron was forged in the territory itself. The fence was added to the property during its early 1970s restoration. The mullioned window was once the location of a small door that was used as the house's main entry.

came the site of the bloody Five Day Battle in February 1878 that ended the Lincoln County War.

The war was fought over the quintessential issues of the American frontier: economic control and political power. Its players and casualties were legion, but the two antagonistic groups were sharply divided into the Murphy-Dolan gang, followers of two powerful and corrupt merchants, and supporters of Alexander McSween, an attorney determined to clean up Lincoln County's economic and political corruption.

The rival groups were by no means the first to come to blows in Lincoln County. Throughout the 1870s, lawlessness was rampant in the area, resulting in frequent loss of life and destruction of property. The Murphy-Dolan and McSween rivalry, however, took the belligerence further, and at the war's

conclusion, the leaders of the losing faction were dead, and the winners were bankrupt.

From its inception, Lincoln County had been the political and economic fiefdom of the mercantile firm of L.G. Murphy and Company. Lawrence Murphy had settled in Lincoln County after 1865 and quickly established a lucrative trade with Fort Stanton. After Murphy's original partner died, a young clerk, J.J. Dolan, rose in the firm's ranks. At the time, Murphy and Company claimed to control men in county offices and the territorial court and boasted of having the backing of high officials. In fact, the company had a reputation for nefarious business practices.

Murphy and Company had very little competition in Lincoln County until 1877, when an idealistic young Englishman,

J.H. Tunstall, built a rival business establishment in Lincoln. Tunstall was aided in his efforts by Alexander A. McSween, an energetic and prosperous lawyer who, by his interest in Republican politics and in cleaning up county corruption, made enemies of the territory's power brokers.

It was the murder of Tunstall on the morning of February 18, 1878, that actually began the Lincoln County War. Tunstall was shot and killed, presumably by a Murphy-Dolan deputy.

Alexander McSween vowed to avenge his friend's death by legal means and to protect his own life and that of his wife. The lines between the two factions were clearly drawn.

Deaths continued on both sides until the Five Day Battle ended in the deaths of McSween, four of his men, and a Murphy-Dolan deputy and the burning of the McSween home on July 19, 1878.

President Rutherford B. Hayes, who sent a special inves-

tigator to New Mexico after Tunstall's shooting, received an informal report on the volatile situation in New Mexico. As a result, he immediately replaced the territorial governor in Santa Fe, but the situation in Lincoln County remained critical. On the anniversary of McSween's murder, his wife's attorney was gunned down in front of her house, finally bringing the new governor and the military district commander to Lincoln. Within two weeks, the surviving lawbreakers were arrested.

English ivy creeps over the fieldstone wall (FAR LEFT). This side of the house, suggestive of New England farmhouses, shows an Anglo influence.

Columbine shoots its sunshine color next to a brick-capped low wall (MIDDLE LEFT). Gentle rolling hills can be seen beyond the native cottonwood trees.

A tall, seventy-inch, double-hung window (NEAR LEFT) is nineteen inches deep.

The Hondo River Valley (ABOVE) is a peaceful setting of mesquite-covered hills and moderate elevations.

In the living room is a late-nineteenth-century drop-leaf pine harvest table from Maine. The blue and white quilt was purchased from two sisters in Santa Fe. The sisters had previously lived near an old shirt factory in Ohio and made the quilt from remnants of shirting fabric. The oil lamp was purchased in an antiques shop; the wooden duck decoys are from Maine. The candlesticks were made from old thread bobbins from a mill in New Hampshire.

This stripped nineteenth-century pine door (ABOVE LEFT) with decorative mill-work leads to the master bedroom.

A black Franklin stove (ABOVE RIGHT) sits in a corner of the living room. The small size of the rolltop desk indicates it was a "lady's" desk, for use at home. Made of oak, it dates from the early twentieth century. The thirteen-star wooden flag is a contemporary piece of folk art.

By the 1880s, Lincoln County had calmed down, and other changes were in the making. By the mid-1890s, the Mescalero Apaches were resettled on reservations, and Fort Stanton was closed. The Santa Fe Railroad had met the Southern Pacific at Deming, New Mexico; in 1881, the transcontinental link across New Mexico was complete. By 1889, the area of Lincoln County began shrinking with political reorganization.

Today the town of Lincoln, home to about sixty people, is no longer the county seat but is a living museum to its rich but troubled past. Thanks to the combined efforts of the Lincoln County Historical Society, a division of the Museum of New Mexico, and the Lincoln County Heritage Trust, visitors can take a walking tour of the town and see restored buildings such as the Courthouse Museum, a two-story adobe built in 1874 by L.G. Murphy and Company.

In 1976 a group of civic-minded cultural and business leaders started the Lincoln County Heritage Trust, a historic preservation group. Among them was Paul Horgan, author of a Pulitzer Prize-winning biography of New Mexico's nineteenth-century archbishop, John Baptist Lamy; Peter Hurd, the late Western artist; Robert O. Anderson, a local rancher and businessman; and John Meigs, a photographer, artist, and designer. The trust acquired and restored historically important houses and buildings in Lincoln that were in private hands and built a local museum. It has also spearheaded what will be a four-summer archeological dig on the site of the burned McSween house.

In the spirit of the restoration efforts of the Lincoln County Heritage Trust, a local businessman and his wife decided to restore a two-story adobe and stone ruin on their Lincoln County ranch in the early 1970s. It is assumed the house was near a stagecoach stop and served as a school in the 1880s and 1890s as well as a home to various local families. Although the precise history of the house has yet to be unearthed by Lincoln County historians, it is suspected that Martin Chavez, a prominent participant in the Lincoln County War and a McSween follower, may have owned the structure and a nearby store.

The house is significant not only because of its role in the early days of Lincoln County, but also because of its unusual adobe and fieldstone construction. Like other buildings in the area, it was influenced by the utilitarian Territorial-style military structures at nearby Fort Stanton. Its pitched roof and box-like design were essentially borrowed from plans drafted by military architects and carried by troops as they advanced west into the frontier. The house, which has been restored with far more elegance than its previous owners could imagine, was soundly constructed, symmetrical, and straightforward in style. In the early days of the county, houses were used as protection. Neither the military nor the settlers wasted money on decorating functional structures. There was no filligree on the portal, the posts were unadorned, and the original doors were small and plain, unlike the carved, multi-paned doors of the Victorian style.

When restoration began, the adobe portion of the house was in serious disrepair; deterioration due to years of neglect, exposure to weather, and a fire in the attic and roof made the restoration of the house a formidable task. The roof joists had to be replaced because of the long-ago fire, but some of the simple tongue-in-groove ceiling escaped fire damage and was saved.

Before restoration, when the owners walked through the first story of the house, they could see the sky through the rotted ceiling boards and the rusted tin roof of the second

In an upstairs bedroom, a contemporary handmade child's dress hangs from an early-nineteenth-century spindle bedstead from Maine. The bed has slats where once ropes held up its mattress. The calico floral quilt on the bed is the "Yo-Yo" pattern; typically these were decorative and not used for warmth. The "Monkey Wrench" quilt on the wall is an early-twentieth-century piece.

floor. They were not able to inspect the second floor at all; banisters were missing from the staircase, as was the second floor landing. Although the present staircase occupies the space of the old one, it has been redesigned and completely rebuilt.

The crumbling adobe of the two-story portion of the house was shored up with iron tie rods called earthquake bolts between the first and second stories to pull the walls together and to give them additional strength. Traditional adobe walls require yearly maintenance, so the house originally had a local lime whitewash applied to its adobe bricks to protect them from exposure to weather. In recent years, builders have often added asphalt emulsion to adobe to increase its strength and durability; in this house, concrete-fortified, adobe-colored plaster was used to cover the bricks and protect the walls from the elements.

The restoration was straightforward, and although more elegant materials were used in the house than there were originally, its simplicity was retained. A new shingle roof replaced the original tin one, and the floors, which were rough pine in some areas and dirt in others, are now wide-planked

To the right of the stairs on the second floor, a blue and white quilt stitched by the owner's Swedish great aunt hangs on the wall (LEFT). It is a variation of the "Double-X" pattern, also known as "Old Maid's Puzzle." A ceramic pitcher and washbowl sit atop a Victorian table.

At the top of the new oak stairs and landing, a nineteenth-century iron washstand and its original pitcher are tucked into the corner (TOP LEFT).

In the master bath (TOP RIGHT), architectural remnants make a delightful turn-of-the-century statement. The marble sink, found in San Francisco, is Victorian. The wood mirror frame is of the same era, but was brought from Maine. The framed needlework is of a Revolutionary War-era soldier.

The white Victorian iron bedstead in the master bedroom (ABOVE) was purchased from an antiques store in Roswell, New Mexico. The marble-topped side pieces are from the early 1920s. The poster announces an exhibition of the paintings of Henriette Wyeth, a Lincoln County neighbor.

oak. The sidecar wainscoting in the living area is original. One-by-four-inch or one-by-six-inch pieces of wood were used in this type of wainscoting and a middle groove milled in the boards to make them seem narrow. Like houses of the era, this one had no closets and plumbing, so a bathroom and closets were added to the two bedrooms upstairs, as well as a bathroom downstairs. The large, homey kitchen was completely rebuilt, but its location is original to the house. Today the house feels simple, cozy, and charming—perfect for its country setting.

A narrow, winding, unpaved drive leading to the house is canopied by a graceful stand of poplars and cottonwoods, both native to the area. The road follows along a narrow, swiftly flowing irrigation ditch of clear water, which feeds nearby fields and the old cottonwood trees growing along its banks. A Victorian wrought-iron fence runs along the east side of the house, and an eighty-foot-long portal ends agreeably in a picket-fence-style trellis on its west end. A neat, rectangular lawn on the south side of the house is enclosed by a plastered, brick-capped low wall. Planted in deep beds along the wall are purple larkspur, columbine, and Shasta daisies, and an enormous elm tree stands court just outside the wall. The view to the south is of tall grasses waving in the wind and of the nearby hills.

Just inside the front door off the south side portal is a short hallway leading to another north-facing door. Along the hallway are pegs for the family's jackets, coats, and riding habits. Framed on the wall just inside the main door is a letter from author Paul Horgan, who wrote portions of his biography of Father Lamy in this house. In the letter, Horgan thanks his hosts for the quiet and solitude he enjoyed while staying in their house.

The interior of the house is furnished in an eclectic mixture of regional styles, which adds immeasurably to its comfortable and practical charm. Family heirlooms are interspersed with other antique pieces and contemporary furniture. Throughout the house, small details or an occasional piece of furniture brings New England to mind, while the overall decor remains firmly Southwestern. A New Mexican trastero sits in the entryway; an 1840 spool bedstead from Maine graces one of the upstairs bedrooms. In the living room, a contemporary but neutral white couch is mixed with old and new in a comfortable, family-oriented room. Quilts and other special details bring to the interiors a peaceful feeling, perfect for a relaxing country house.

A contemporary star-patterned quilt brightens the table at the end of the south portal. Casual benches provide seating beneath a trellis planted with Virginia creeper and English ivy, which is inching its way along the exposed fieldstone wall of the house's one-story section.

CONTEMPORARY TERRITORIAL
ATTENTION TO DETAIL
IN OLD SANTA FE

A meandering pathway of flagstone and native rock draws visitors into the naturally landscaped front garden (LEFT), which is planted with shady cottonwood trees, wildflowers, and sprawling ground cover. A portal shades the doorway, which is festooned with chiles. A flat roof covers some of the wings. Such flat roofs are bowed up in the center, allowing melting snow or rainwater to run off into canales, or drain spouts.

Two carved mythological creatures greet guests at the front doorway (RIGHT).

At first glance, the streets in the old section of Santa Fe seem to loop and wind haphazardly, converging at eight-way intersections, then radiating outward like the leaves of an agave. Perhaps the Pueblo Indians, the Spanish colonists, or the early Anglo settlers had their reasons and destinations for which these twisting roadways were created, but those reasons are lost to time. Today the town's winding avenues have a greater purpose: to slow the pace and to charm drivers and pedestrians alike with the fascinating architecture of Santa Fe.

Everywhere in the center of the old town, there are intriguing adobe houses whose mysterious high walls protect secret gardens and prevent peeks at rambling cottages.

One such contemporary adobe hidden from the street by a softly rounded, plastered garden wall belongs to June Josey. She bought it because she admired its design and the dimensions were perfect for her needs. But her true reasons for acquiring the house were more subliminal—Santa Fe in general and this house in particular enchanted her, and the narrow stream that ran through the garden captivated her.

Perhaps most of the magical magnetism of the house can be credited to its builder, noted Santa Fe designer Betty Stewart, who shaped mud, tin, bricks, wood, and plaster into a simple, elegant architectural statement evocative of the traditional Territorial style.

A descendent of several generations of Texas ranchers, Betty Stewart began her career in residential adobe design and construction in the early 1970s, when she had her own house built of the local sand and clay bricks. She found the experience so enriching that she went on to build dozens of residences in the piñon-studded high desert of northern New Mexico, each of them bearing her purist attention to detail.

The time period the designer's work draws upon is the Territorial era, from the mid-1800s to the early twentieth century, when New Mexico was annexed by the United States. The opening of the Santa Fe Trail and later the railroad brought an increasing Anglo influence to the culture—and architecture—of Santa Fe, intertwining with that of the Indians and the Spanish colonists. The organically shaped Pueblo style of architecture were spruced up with modern ornamentation: glass for windows, milled lumber, red bricks, simple columns. Floor plans became more structured, organized.

The original site of the Josey house had been occupied by a deteriorated 150-year-old one-room adobe. It had no plumbing or wiring and its doors were little more than cardboard. The lot, however, was generous in size—almost three-quarters of an acre—and was close to the shops, art galleries, and restaurants that flavor the town. The soothing trickle of the Acequia Madre, an ancient irrigation canal, cooled one edge of the garden. Instead of bulldozing the old house, the designer chose to incorporate it into the new structure.

The house Betty Stewart built epitomizes her style and technique. Working around the existing adobe, she created a 3,300-square-foot house with two spacious bedrooms, a central kitchen, an entry gallery, and an airy great room, a perfect name for the room that serves as both living and dining areas. A portal from one side of the great room connects to an outdoor fireplace, extending the living space into nature when weather permits.

To protect it from the warm summer sun and the crisp, sometimes snowy winter months, the house is built with double adobe walls, which are separated by several inches of airspace for insulation. The adobe bricks—a combination of

Weather permitting, the shaded patio (LEFT) becomes an outdoor extension of the great room. The table is an antique French pastry table; the ceramic piece above the fireplace is a small lantern. The wooden fencing behind the house, made from saplings, is known as a coyote fence. Early settlers devised this impenetrable, tall barrier to ensure the safety of their livestock from the carnivorous animals.

From the side garden, the symmetrical simplicity of this Territorial-style adobe house is evident (TOP). Refined details, such as the mullioned windows and brick trim, are typical of Territorial-style architecture.

Pitched tin roofs are common in northern New Mexico, which receives more precipitation than the low-lying southern deserts. The house is constructed with a double roof (ABOVE), for extra insulation.

sand and clay—are made locally. A double insulated roof also keeps the temperature constant within.

The beauty of the house is in the details; they work together subtly to create a sense of stateliness that is not often associated with adobe styles of architecture. In this area, Betty Stewart enforces her well-researched standards, even down to the types of tools she allows her crews to use during construction. She eschews the bulbous beehive fireplaces, the excessive niches, and other regrettably overused touches that have cropped up in crudely worked new Pueblo or Territorial styles.

A portion of the house is capped by a pitched red tin roof, a very traditional style in northern New Mexico where rain and snow are facts of life. The flat roofs—common in hotter, drier parts of the state, and in Pueblo architecture—become nothing more than "swimming pools" in Santa Fe, the designer explains. To prevent the design of the Josey house from becoming too cluttered, she did use a form of flat roof over the back wing, but it is elevated in the center. Water runs off in carved wooden canales, or drain spouts.

Additionally, the home has the crisp, sharp edges more distinctive of the Territorial style, not the hand-molded, rounded corners of the Pueblo, or Santa Fe, style. Brick coping on the adobe parapets and on the chimneys adds yet another reminder of the style's era. Nonetheless, the home retains its handcrafted look because the designer prohibits her crew from using levels. Walls are whimsically bowed; splayed window reveals, which scatter brilliant light into the rooms, are charmingly crooked.

Inside and out, plaster was hand applied over the adobe bricks. The rosy sand color of the exterior and the pearly white of the interior were mixed into the plaster. Betty Stewart's greatest sleight of hand, however, occurred in the interior walls. Using a secret plaster mixture and troweling technique,

Looking from the great room, the gallery (TOP RIGHT) is lit with morning sun. Old bricks set in sand were used as flooring, and interspersed throughout the house are old vigas collected over the years by the designer. The saddle is the owner's, dating back to her childhood on her parents' Texas ranch; the portrait above it is by New Orleans artist Joe Bernstein. The wooden statue of St. George and the Dragon is an Italian antique.

A bombe in the corner of the gallery (BOTTOM RIGHT) is topped by a terracotta Florentine bust wearing a necklace—one of the owner's more tongue-in-cheek arrangements. The doors to the great room are New Mexican antiques, and the light fixture is from Mexico.

58

A skylight gently illuminates the kitchen, where a curved, raised fireplace is the focal point. The marble-topped table and wrought-iron chairs are antique garden furnishings. The "cat" cupboard was made by a Taos craftsman; the red chair was painted by Peter Hunt, a contemporary Pennsylvania Dutch artist. The light fixtures are tin, as is the antique horse from a French butcher's shop.

The mantelpiece (FAR LEFT) for the great room is carved from one piece of pine and hand pegged. Pewter mantel items found in London are Art Nouveau.

The vaulted ceiling in the great room (LEFT) creates a feeling of volume, and the window reveals have a formal arch. June Josey found that her collection of antiques fit perfectly in her Santa Fe home. The portrait is of the owner's father, painted by Gerard de Rose; the bronze statue in the window is German. The box below the portrait is a Chinese parchment chest. The dried flower wreath above the fireplace was made at a shop in Santa Fe. The candlesticks on either side of the fireplace are Italian.

At one end of the room sits a desk for reading and letter writing (ABOVE). The owner found it at an antiques shop in Dallas and had an artist friend adorn it with faux leopard spots. The antique terra-cotta statue is French; the chair is Venetian; the portrait is English. The fruitwood bibliothèque, topped by a collection of primitive African masks, stretches across one wall of the great room and has become an architectural element in itself.

61

she produced a wall surface that is smooth and luminous, not unlike old Spanish frescoes. Light bounces and sparkles off the walls.

Throughout the house, more personal touches are evident. Antique bricks set in sand provide handsome flooring for the great room, kitchen, and gallery. In the bedrooms, the designer refinished the existing honey-colored pine floors and added new planks where the space was extended. On the ceilings, she put to use her collection of age-worn vigas, adzed by hand. She also installed several antique New Mexican doors and beautiful wooden fireplace mantels. She used mullioned windows, neatly sectioning the views from the

house into the lush garden. In the kitchen and bathrooms, the painted pine cabinetry and handcrafted doors are new, yet unobtrusive.

Betty Stewart had barely finished building the house when a local resident purchased it from her. The woman who lived there for several years added a discreet garage and landscaped the front courtyard in a natural style, shaded by cottonwood trees and sparked with day lilies and native wildflowers.

When June Josey acquired the house, one of the many things she noticed was that the interior architecture was classic, enduring. The house, despite its Santa Fe roots, was remi-

Layered antique linens, a down comforter, and an upholstered Angelo Donghia bed are creature comforts in the master bedroom (LEFT). The aged wood lintel above the door is typical of the designer's style.

A small fireplace is angled in a corner of the master bedroom (ABOVE). The mantelpiece, made of old pine, was handmade by a local craftsman. The owner has added some of her personal treasures, including a Victorian fireplace screen, a profile of a child painted by her mother, and juggling pins used by her father to stay in shape.

niscent of dwellings in the hills of northern Italy or the fragrant meadows of Provence. With its straightforward lines, the house provides an excellent foil for a variety of furniture periods and styles.

For June Josey, it was the perfect match. Few of her pieces are Southwestern, but her collection of French antiques—many of which have been in her family for years—complement the house well. At one end of the great room, a recamier, a Regency armchair, and a French cheese table make a comfortable grouping in front of the fireplace. In another corner of the room, an old desk, adorned with faux leopard spots, is angled between a window and an imposing

fruitwood bibliothèque. An old cupboard, handpainted by a Pennsylvania Dutch artist, is a focal point in the gallery.

The owner did the interior design herself, trusting her own sense of personal style and the integrity of her furnishings. "I just don't take decorating seriously," she says. "It should be fun." Feather boas are draped over mirrors, inexpensive necklaces ornament serious-looking busts, a violet-hued fox throw hugs the recamier. An avid reader and world traveler, June Josey has collected history, art, and travel books that cheerfully fill cupboards, shelves, tables, and any other available surface. The resulting interior is lively and as charming as the exterior and the gardens.

Splayed, deep-set window reveals (FAR LEFT) spread light into the house. The thickness of the outer walls is readily apparent. A special plaster mixture and troweling technique give the interior walls their fresco-like sheen. The architectural fragment is probably Italian, fourteenth century. The books are old travel tomes about Spain.

This ancient irrigation canal, the Acequia Madre, slices through one edge of the garden (LEFT). Wooden steps allow visitors to test the waters.

The cow skull (ABOVE) was found on the Texas ranch where the owner grew up. The exterior plaster of the house was hand troweled, and the color mixed into the plaster.

65

ABSTRACTED TRADITIONAL

A MOUNTAIN OF FORMS RISES FROM THE TAOS MESA

The "high road" to the small town of Taos from Santa Fe takes a tranquil, leisurely route through historic little communities such as Chimayo, with its jewel-like ancient santuario, or sanctuary. By contrast, on the main road to Taos, the mighty Rio Grande makes its dramatic presence known.

As the Rio Grande flows into New Mexico from Colorado, it travels through a deep gorge for some forty-eight miles, its normally placid waters becoming frenzied as it pushes southward. The bright, rushing water near Taos is 650 feet below the wide, flat sagebrush plain.

The area around Taos, which lies at the foot of the Sangre de Cristo Range (literally, "the blood of Christ"), was settled by local Indians probably as early as A.D. 900. The Indian name for Taos is Tua-tah, meaning "our village." A soldier with the Spanish explorer Coronado, Captain Hernando Alvarado, visited here in 1540, and soon the Spanish influence was in Taos to stay. The ancient Tiwa-speaking Indian culture still flourishes at Taos Pueblo, a traditional Indian village of 2,000 situated about three miles northeast of town.

Sunlight penetrates the covered portico on the east side of the house (LEFT). Simple willow furniture lines the walls.

A dramatic processional stairway (RIGHT) on the south side invites exploration and completes the north-south axis of the house. The roof is metal, a deliberate response to local architecture, in which tin roofs are common. The zinc-coated steel will oxidize and weather over time to reflect the blue and gray colors of the sky.

The spun gold of New Mexican sunlight reaches through stormy skies on the mesa in Taos to illuminate the man-made addition to the existing mountain forms.

Exterior windows are trimmed with a ribbon of Taos blue, a color traditionally used by the Spanish to ward off evil spirits (LEFT).

Steps to the second-level terrace and a square window play with the surrounding walls to form abstract composition of sunlight and shadow (RIGHT).

The heart of the town of Taos is its plaza, dating from 1710, with its low adobe buildings and wide porches. Around the plaza or at the Taos Book Store, local residents still refer to "Mabel and Tony's house" as if time has stood still for fifty years. Mabel was Mabel Dodge Luhan, a New York writer and heiress who came to Taos in 1917 and later married a local Taos Indian, Tony Luhan. Her friends, among them the English writer D.H. Lawrence and his wife, Frieda, writer-critic Carl Van Vechten and English portrait painter Lady Dorothy Brett, were summoned by this formidable restless spirit to Taos and helped to foster an intellectual and creative atmosphere that still draws writers and artists from all over the world to its mesas and mountains.

Even before this time, two artists, Bert Phillips and Ernest Blumenschein, who were on a wide-ranging sketching trip from Denver to Mexico City in 1898, stopped at Taos Pueblo. They were enchanted by the landscape and the Pueblo Indians and stayed to begin the Taos Art Colony. They exhibited their Taos paintings all over the country and popularized the area.

Other painters quickly followed. In 1914 the Taos Society of Artists was formed and held exhibitions in New York, Bos-

In the sunny main hall (ABOVE), a wide oak stairway leads to the bedroom level. The warm terra-cotta color of the second-story walls is the same used to detail many of the exterior doorways.

Windows and doors allow diners to share in a view which has inspired generations of visual artists. In the formal thirty-five-foot dining room (RIGHT), is a nine-foot, nineteenth-century English cherry table purchased in New Orleans. The ornate chairs are twentieth-century reproductions. They are upholstered with a dusty rose fabric that compliments the old Tabriz rug on the floor.

The warm light in the formal living area at night illuminates an elegant mix of antique, contemporary, and Southwestern furnishings (LEFT).

This dried flower arrangement sits atop the dining room table in a pot made by Mexico's Tarahumara Indians (ABOVE).

ton, and Philadelphia. Word of Taos spread to Europe, attracting well-known painters from Russia, Austria, and England. Taos is still rich in art and artists. R.C. Gorman, the celebrated Navajo painter, sculptor, and printmaker, lives and works in a restored old adobe home.

The small area is a confluence of Indian, Spanish, and Anglo cultures. The 3,000 permanent residents of the town of Taos are predominantly Spanish, and ancient controversies among its ethnic groups about issues such as water rights persist to this day.

Just north of town, the Hondo River flows through a small community on its way to join the Rio Grande. Here, the even, broad mesa plays with the clear sky and surrounding mountains. The Jemez Mountains, Truchas Peak, the volcanic dome of San Antonio Mountain, and Vallecito Mountain are in stark view on what was originally a sagebrush plain in the area near the small community of Arroyo Hondo. After years of irrigation, the sagebrush has given way to wavy, luminescent alfalfa, and it is here that Nat and Connie Troy of Louisiana found the ideal site for their vacation home.

The Troys had been coming to Taos for winter skiing and summer vacations for more than a decade when they decided they wanted more privacy and space than their condominium in the Taos ski valley provided. They knew they wanted uninterrupted views immersed in the clear Taos light and enough land to raise quarter horses. What they found was a twenty-acre site on the mesa, adjacent to a 1,400-acre ranch.

"It was the panoramic view that attracted us," says Nat Troy. "You can see the mountains to the east, and you can see forever to the west."

To translate their wishes for their Southwestern home into reality, the Troys consulted with Albuquerque architect Antoine Predock. His work in Taos was well known to the couple, and after telling him they wanted views, decks, ample access to the outdoors, and spacious rooms flowing from one to the other, they gave the architect free rein.

When he first saw the site for the Troys new home, Predock was struck with its stark beauty. Wind and lack of moisture keep everything on the mesa close to the earth, so the relationship of the flat land to the mountains is quite powerful.

"It was very important to mark a place on the landscape," says Predock. "There was nothing to snuggle up against, as in the ski valley. I saw the house as an archi-

tectural event on the landscape, standing alone, but also as part of its environment."

The design of the house is an abstraction of the surrounding landscape, especially of the mountains to the west. The imagery is of a generalized, mountain-like form, angled on the north and south sides, with the multiple layerings of a mesa. From an aerial perspective, the house looks simple and geometric, but from any one of a dozen different angles, it is an aesthetically pleasing visual puzzle.

Seen from the horizon or as one approaches from its long driveway, the house appears to be a monolith. It is earth-bermed on its north side, giving it a peaked form. A stairway marches up the berm, "an architectural completion of the slope," in the architect's view, "to engage the family to explore the house." The packed earth is planted with alfalfa and wildflowers and in spring and summer is solid green with small shocks of color. Stairs on the south side complete the home's north-south axis.

Upon closer look, a bright, shiny roof shoots out, echoing the slope of the berm. The metal roof is a major design element of the frame construction house, and its material—zinc-coated steel—is reminiscent of local tin roofing and its color will weather and reflect the colors of the sky.

The north stairway leads to the house's bedroom level, which corresponds to a second floor, and the south exterior staircase, precisely at the same level and angle, completes the idea of ingress and egress. The 4,500-square-foot house has many levels and is wrapped with layers of decks that add 3,000 square feet of space, making the house look much larger. The decks provide the Troys with multiple entries to the outside from within the house.

An Irish country cupboard works well with an English soft pine table in the expansive kitchen. Geese prance on a metal chandelier above the table; both were purchased in a Dallas antiques store. The specially crafted kitchen cabinets are pine.

A late-nineteenth-century Austrian piano (RIGHT) was chosen to be the focus of the formal living area. The room's stepped adobe fireplace, handcrafted by a local Taos artisan, makes a dramatic cruciform architectural statement. The tongue-in-groove fir ceiling peaks to thirty-two feet.

A view from the balcony of the den (FAR RIGHT) reveals the restrained but elegant approach of the design for the living area, where the adobe fireplace is juxtaposed with an Oriental rug, contemporary white couch, and the Austrian piano. There are some 8,000 square feet of terra-cotta-colored concrete tile inside and outside the house. The tiles were crafted in New Mexico.

74

Light and shadow change with the season and the time of day, creating vast differences in the way the exterior of the house is perceived. At first glance the house looks unabashedly contemporary. When viewed from different planes and angles, however, it becomes clear that the architect placed the house firmly in its setting and within New Mexican architectural traditions. He transformed traditional elements in a way that he calls "innovation, not reiteration." The house has Territorial-style adobe aspects, with stepped angles and straight lines, as well as Pueblo-style influences, which give a feeling of solidity and village-like aggregation of forms. The material chosen for the frame-constructed house was plaster, not adobe, because the Troys wanted two stories and wide-open views. Although they felt adobe was not an appropriate building material, they made the wall studs extra wide to give an adobe-like thick wall effect for both style and insulation.

After winter had passed and the Troys saw their new home for the first time in the soft, clear light of spring, they suspected someone had changed its color. The original exterior had been painted in three different earth tones of the mesa: buckskin, cottonwood, and fawn. The integrally colored stucco was created by mixing pigment with plaster and sand to give depth to the color. The final look, with its nuances of light, is quite different from the appearance of paint. The Troys were astounded at how different the house looked to them in the light of the new season.

Other colorations and their effects are evident in the detailing of exterior windows and doors. Many doors are emblazoned with terra-cotta, and a number of windows are trimmed in Taos blue, a clear, deep azure traditionally used in the area by the Spanish people to keep evil spirits out. Exterior windows on the west side of the house, for example, are

placed in a wall painted the pale fawn color. A plump square of white frames the window, with a ribbon of Taos blue within the white frame. Below the window, the color changes to the brighter cottonwood.

The approach to the house is from the east, through a wooden gate to a wood-columned portico covered by a trellis. The entry was designed as a transition passage, built on a low plane and aimed at the horizon to capture mountain views. The passageway ends in a twelve-by-sixteen-foot grass square. To the left are massive oak entry doors; to the right is the entrance to the Troys' guest house.

The doors lead into an open interior that rises to the bedroom level. A wide oak stairwell faces the entryway. The Troys are collectors of contemporary and traditional Southwestern art, and paintings and pieces of sculpture are everywhere. The interior is decorated with a combination of American and European antiques; there are contemporary pieces as well, and some unmistakably whimsical interpretations of New Mexican rustic.

To the immediate left on the ground floor is the master suite. The terra-cotta color of the exterior detailing sweeps inside and is found on the walls surrounding the master suite door and follows the stairs up to the three bedrooms on the second level.

Following the entryway and then turning to the right a short distance is an interior portal that follows the north-south axis of the house on the lower level.

An informal den is found to the left of the passageway; it has a planked ceiling with traditional vigas and shares a remarkable stepped adobe fireplace with the open living room, where a tongue-in-groove fir ceiling soars to thirty-two feet at its apex. The fireplace, designed by the architect, was executed by local craftspeople.

The interior portal ends in a loft-like space with wonderful mountain views. The dining room is found opposite the

---

The low plane of the passageway to the house (FAR LEFT) creates a ceremonial feeling, with its simple slatted covering and vertical posts. It is aimed at the mountain view of the western horizon. The sculpted fountain by Albuquerque artist Kit Schweitzer is called "The Watersong."

A few small steps on the upper level (LEFT) lead to the second-floor terrace and to the bedrooms. Views beckon to the mountains and mesa beyond the house's perimeter as sunlight partially illuminates a boldly painted terra-cotta interior wall.

living room. Four enormous terra-cotta pots brimming with red geraniums sit on the floor on the south side of the room. The dining room shares back-to-back fireplaces with the open, light-filled kitchen, which has double multi-paned doors and looks out across the mesa to the Rio Grande Gorge to the west. Beyond the kitchen is a spacious laundry room and "mud" room where family members can change from riding or ski clothes to less rugged attire.

Up the oak stairway to the bedroom level is a small sitting area called the solarium. Surrounded by multiple second-story windows, one can see the full panorama of mountains and mesa in a 360-degree view. The area is furnished with two armchairs and a small table.

Aligned on the south side of the house on the second level are two bedrooms, bath, and den, which follow along the upper north-south axis of the house. The den, which doubles as a fourth bedroom, is open on its south wall and overlooks the living room. An exterior door opposite the den leads to the upper level terrace and a small fireplace. On the southeast corner of the upper outdoor level is what the owner calls "the most strategically placed hot tub in the world." Bathers can look to the south, west, and east at some of the most beautiful high country anywhere.

The ground floor portal wrapping around the south side of the house was designed as a protected space where the family can enjoy their summer sojourns in Taos. The portal was carefully designed so that the low winter sun can fill the house with light during winter ski vacations.

The interiors were planned with Warren Ringheim, a Louisiana interior designer. Antiques shops and art galleries in the South and Southwest were scoured for most of a year, and often a room's interior was created around a single piece of furniture or work of art. The dining room, for example, was designed around a tapestry by R.C. Gorman. The large, eight-by-five-foot tapestry, "Gossiping Women," which hangs above the dining room fireplace, is strong in rose tones, and rose fabric covering the dining room chairs complements the tapestry.

A fierce wind can come up fast on the mesa. The alfalfa blows freely in the wind and then, quite abruptly, the wind stops and peace reigns again on the plain beneath the mountains. The Troys are enchanted with the house and with the beauty of Taos. "When you see the sun in the early mornings," says Nat Troy, "it is impossible to sleep late. You are duty-bound to get up and look at all this beauty."

In an upstairs bedroom an early-twentieth-century quilt covers a painted iron bed. The hand-painted bench is the work of Taos artist Jim Wagner.

TEXAS

A lone man on horseback, riding tall in the saddle, gallops across the dusty, desolate desert and saves the ranch. Throw in a ten-gallon hat and a few cholla cacti, and the common image of Texas is formed. But the Lone Star state, all 267,000 square miles of it, cannot be painted in a single brushstroke. Its geography, its history, and most certainly its architecture are subtle mosaics; examined closely, they reveal there really is not one Texas. Instead, the state is a fascinating pastiche—perhaps a microcosm of the United States itself.

In Texas three major geographic subdivisions of North America do a do-si-do: the Rocky Mountains, the Great Plains, and the Gulf Coastal Forested Plains. The result is a topography that features benign, wildflower-carpeted prairies, flat, scorching deserts, dense forests, swamps, and miles of beach. It is a state where weathermen can predict a hurricane and a record snowfall during the same newscast.

This varied topography was roamed by handfuls of Indians long before Europeans or Americans claimed the land. Those in the eastern portion of the state had life a bit easier than their cousins to the west. Bountiful forests provided them with the wood and grasses to build semi-permanent thatch-roof huts, and the rich soil allowed them to have an agrarian existence. Some of these Indian tribes built vast dirt mounds, pyramids with log stairs, presumably used for worship. To the west, the tribes were more nomadic, living in hide-covered tepees and following herds of buffalo, which provided them with sustenance. Along the Rio Grande valley, also in the west, the Pueblo culture flourished. The Indians coaxed beans and squash out of a rather inhospitable earth and built great stone and mud dwellings that housed many families.

As elsewhere throughout the Southwest, the Spaniards were the first Europeans to explore Texas. They gave the state its name, taking an Indian word, tejas, meaning "friend" or "friendly." As early as 1519, the explorer Alvarez de Piñeda made his way up the Gulf coast from Florida into Texas. Inland, Juan de Oñate pushed through the western part of the state. Oñate brought with him not only arms, but domesticated mustangs and cattle as well. The natives, however, were somewhat less than friendly to the Spaniards. Marred by Indian hostilities in the New World, Spain's glory days were also waning in Europe by the end of the seventeenth century. In the meantime, the French explorer La Salle tiptoed into Texas. Returning to North America after one successful exploration, La Salle was sailing for Louisiana when a wrong turn led him to the Texas coast. The year was 1685, and La Salle hoisted the fleur-de-lis, honoring his king, Louis XIV.

Spurred into action by the French, the Spaniards vowed to secure Texas for the crown by establishing missions and colonies. From the late 1600s through most of the eighteenth century, the Franciscans supervised the building of some thirty-six missions, stretching from the Rio Grande almost to Louisiana. Skilled Spanish craftsmen were imported to run crews of Indians, most of whom had no building skills. Materials used for the missions included adobe blocks, but much of Texas was also rich in native stone. In those areas limestone, sandstone, and granite were often layered in with the adobe bricks in the construction of a wall; a whiter limestone was frequently used for facades and decorative trim. The missionaries emulated the ecclesiastical styles favored in Spain: Romanesque vaults, cruciform floor plans, embellished doorways and windows, brightly colored frescoes. Of the missions, perhaps Mission San Antonio de Valero—the Alamo—has become the most famous for its secular use as the scene of a famous battle.

Near the missions the Spanish colonists used the jacal method of constructing shelters, which consisted of sinking log posts vertically into the ground, then filling the gaps with mud. In the deserts these shelters were usually crude adobe hovels because wood was not readily available.

By the early nineteenth century Spanish control over the New World had weakened; Mexico gained its independence—and control over the territory of Texas. During that period Mexico set up colonization laws to encourage the settlement of Texas. Immigrants from the United States, primarily the Middle Atlantic states, and Europe, as well as Mexicans filtered into Texas, where land was cheap and the class system nonexistent. To settle Texas, the immigrants had to become Mexican citizens and embrace Catholicism. For the settlers from the United States, these and other regulations eventually caused great discord. Because of its own internal battles the fledgling government of Mexico was unable to manage its northern lands. As the Anglo population increased in Texas, more troubles arose.

By 1835 the "Texians" went to battle with Mexico. Several bloody battles later, including the siege at the Alamo, Texas became an independent republic. Sam Houston, who led the battle for independence, became its first president. Texas remained a republic for nine years and in 1845 became the twenty-eighth state. During the Civil War it became a part of the Confederacy; historically, the state was as much a part of the Old South as it was the Wild West.

During the first half of the nineteenth century, a variety of settlers poured into Texas, bringing with them their cultural traditions—and their architectural styles. Americans, Germans, Slavs, Scandinavians, and some French settled different regions; the Hispanic and Indian cultures had their strongholds as well.

The Scandinavians and especially the Germans, who were skilled as stonemasons, built protective rock houses in their settlements. *Fachwerk* dwellings, which were half rock, half timber, were another Germanic import. Built according to age-old methods, these rock houses were adapted to the frontier and furnished simply with handmade furniture. Another German innovation was the "Sunday house," a concept common throughout the nineteenth century. Country residents built tiny frame houses in town to give their families a place to stay when they came in for church or supplies. The homes often had a sleeping attic for the children.

In the cattle country of western Texas, ranch houses also flourished. Built of adobe or stone, they usually had a pitched roof that extended over the front and back of the house. Most of them were only one room deep to provide good cross ventilation in the desert regions.

It was in the mid-1800s that architecture in the state began to reflect Texas's economic prosperity. Cotton and cattle were important industries, and railroads soon crisscrossed the state. In the southeast huge Greek Revival mansions on the plantations spoke of graceful hospitality—and money. In the western cattle areas humble ranch houses were also dressed up with carved shutters, fancy glasswork, and wooden pediments as if to deny Hispanic influences. In Galveston, located on the Gulf, businessmen built lavish palaces in a variety of classical styles. Some even had their houses designed and built in sections on the Eastern seaboard, then shipped around Florida for assembly on-site in Texas.

By the end of the nineteenth century, Victoriana was in full bloom throughout the state. Furnishings became more elaborate as shipping them became easier. Queen Anne, Eastlake and Carpenter Gothic style houses sprang up in major towns, each one a quaintly elaborate wedding cake of turrets, gables, and lacy wood trim.

At the turn of the century, a major oil field was discovered and the Texas boom began. With the oil industry, mercantile and real estate ventures also began to flourish throughout Texas. Cities developed at a rapid pace. Dallas and Houston, once small dots on the landscape, became major urban centers after World War II. Construction happened everywhere, and architects found commissions were plentiful. Bruce Goff, Frank Lloyd Wright, and others left their marks on residences; some chose to build mansions reminiscent of antebellum times. I. M. Pei, Louis Kahn, Mies van der Rohe, Philip Johnson, and the firm of Skidmore, Owings and Merrill changed the skyline of Texas cities.

From a sparsely settled territory, Texas has evolved into a well-populated and economically powerful state. Its "style" has also developed in a myriad of directions. No doubt the diversity will continue, as long as there is Lone Star pride.

ROCK RANCH

HOME ON THE RANGE IN THE HILLS OF ALPINE

Home, sweet home on the range. Southwestern Texas surely must have been the inspiration for that traditional American folksong. Here vast, uninterrupted stretches of arid grassland dizzy first-time visitors. Cotton-puff clouds dot hard blue skies, and the sunshine is dazzling, unyielding. The buffalo may be long gone, but the deer and the antelope do play.

In the midst of this big country is the small town of Alpine, nestled nearly a mile high in the Davis Mountains, where the folks are friendly and fast-food chains have yet to standardize the community. The area in which Alpine is situated, just north of the Rio Grande, was first settled by Anglos in the mid-1800s. The first settlers tried to eke out a living ranching and mining but soon found themselves impeded in their efforts by raiding Comanches and Apaches. To the north of Alpine, Fort Davis was established in 1854 to protect the settlers and assure safe passage for the Butterfield Overland Mail, which careened through the territory on its way from St. Louis to California.

By the 1880s the Indians had been subdued, and Alpine

The ranch house (LEFT) was built of native rock and mortar in the 1920s. A new rock and frame wing, added in recent years, was constructed to blend with the simple homespun design of the original rock structure.

These old bells were once used to announce the arrival of wagons, but now they decorate a weathered fence post (RIGHT).

A hogback mesa glows with the first light of dawn. The geologic formation was so named because its outcroppings and ridges resemble the bony back of a javelina.

A spectacular sunrise above the McIntyre-Morrow Ranch (LEFT).

Horses roam peacefully in a pasture near the ranch house (FAR LEFT).

The new wing (ABOVE) is centered around a spacious informal family room, decorated in a more contemporary style than the rest of the house. Carol Morrow upholstered the bench of the window seat and made matching cushions; the needlepoint pillows were done by Vivian McIntyre. The drawing of the Hereford cattle is by local artist Wayne Baize, and the collection of old crockery, found in and around some of the ranch buildings, adds a decorative accent. The expanse of windows overlook the front yard and the pasture.

When the original house was constructed, the living room fireplace (LEFT) was built first. The spurs and guns belong to Mo Morrow. The drawing of the burros is by local artist Wayne Baize.

was established as a cattle and sheep ranching area. It was said that the town was named by a young woman who had recently returned from a grand tour of the Continent. She thought that the high elevation and mountains were vaguely reminiscent of the Alps. When the Santa Fe and Southern Pacific railroads chugged through town in the late 1800s, Alpine's population grew. Today ranching is still very much a family affair and a major industry. Beef, in the form of Hereford cattle, is king.

In a shady valley just outside town is the headquarters of one such large family operation, the McIntyre-Morrow Ranch. With its native stone and mortar main house, the ranch has maintained its Western charm through three generations. Its serenity has sheltered and nurtured family togetherness. Today its present owners—the third generation—have added some contemporary conveniences to make rural lifestyle even sweeter.

Mo and Carol Morrow came to live at the main house of the ranch several years ago, when Mo Morrow returned to Alpine to join his father in the family ranching business. Born in the town, he had left to attend college and then lived for a while in Austin. His late grandparents, Vivian and Vernon McIntyre, had started the ranch and built the stone house in

The Morrows updated the kitchen not long after they moved in, adding new cabinetry, flooring, and appliances (ABOVE LEFT). The counters are higher than average because the Morrows are both tall. To show off the McIntyre family crystal collection, a glass-front cabinet was built, edged in stained glass by Karen Williams, a local Alpine artist. The cabinet holds Fostoria and Waterford pieces. The eggs are courtesy of the ranch hens.

To add more space to the kitchen, a wall was knocked out and an outdoor patio enclosed, creating a breakfast room (ABOVE). The oak cupboard, chairs, and round table are practical and rugged. The quilt on the chair was made by Mo Morrow's grandmother; the doilies on the cupboard were done by his wife's mother and sister. Shafford's "Blue Ducks" is a contemporary porcelain pattern. The potted African violets are probably thirty years old.

The furnishings in the dining room (ABOVE), as well as in most of the other rooms, date back to the 1920s, when Mo Morrow's grandparents first moved into the house. His grandmother, a well-traveled woman and renowned hostess, enjoyed collecting china and crystal, such as these Royal Doulton "Clifton" and "Prelude" china patterns, the Fostoria crystal, sterling goblets, and monogrammed flatware. She also crocheted the lace tablecloth.

the 1920s. His mother was born and raised in the house, then moved to town when she married.

As elsewhere in the United States, the rock house genre has existed in Texas for generations. Its heritage can be traced easily to Europe. Stone and masonry houses were first popular among the large group of German immigrants who were brought to the free Republic of Texas in the 1830s and 1840s, under the patronage of a group of German noblemen. They translated their half-timber, half-masonry *Fachwerk* architecture into a frontier vernacular. Although the settlers brought with them detailed knowledge of building techniques, they found that the wilderness forced them to adapt. In areas of little timber, their houses were built mostly of native stone.

Although the McIntyres were not of German descent, they chose to build their simple, rectangular house of native rock, which was plentiful on the ranch property. As a building material, it retained warmth in the winter months and kept out heat in the summer.

Mo Morrow spent many childhood weekends at his

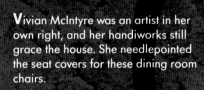

Vivian McIntyre was an artist in her own right, and her handiworks still grace the house. She needlepointed the seat covers for these dining room chairs.

In the master bedroom furnishings from the 1920s and a quilt made by Vivian McIntyre of scraps from old dresses are gentle reminders of by-gone times. She also needlepointed the cover for the footstool. The rose wall color is original; the trim was newly painted for contrast.

grandparents' ranch. The days were filled with games, laughter, conversations, parties, and celebrations. Swings hung from oak and cedar trees; indoors, there were dominoes and other games for the grandchildren. He learned to hunt and ride, and by the time he was a teenager, he learned more about ranching: fixing windmills, mending fences, branding, rounding up cattle, caring for sick animals. By that time, his father was also deeply involved in the family ranch. Frequently the three generations would all rise at dawn and work until well after dark.

During their lifetime, the McIntyres entertained frequently at the ranch. It was not unusual for them to invite more than a hundred people for a real Texas-style barbecue. Vivian McIntyre, an energetic and stylish woman, spearheaded the local USO during the 1940s. She traveled the world, collecting the delicate china and crystal that she used while hosting teas and other social functions. Her home was a gracious counterpoint to rugged life on the ranch. She quilted, crocheted, and did needlepoint, decorating her home in a genteel manner.

When Mo Morrow and his wife Carol, a physical education teacher, decided to live at the ranch house not long after they were married, family memories were not enough for their present lifestyle. The simple house, shaded by mature trees, was in good condition, but it had not been remodeled since the 1940s. The floor plan—three bedrooms, formal living and dining rooms—had fit the needs of the previous generations but was inadequate for the young couple. Keeping in mind the architectural lines of the one-story rock house, they chose to remodel portions of the interior and to add a wing.

Working with a local contractor, they first tackled the kitchen, which was too small for their needs. A sunny breakfast alcove was added, greatly expanding the space. Using her instinctive design talents, Carol Morrow sought to create an informal, warm country look that complemented the rest of the house. She chose white cabinets with traditional lines and had glass doors installed on some to display part of Vivian McIntyre's crystal collection. Deep green flooring, which shows off a group of rag rugs, a wood-burning stove (used for warmth, not cooking), and new appliances and countertops, helped to bring the kitchen up-to-date.

After completing the kitchen, they turned a small, dark home office into an airy family room with a high ceiling. In one corner a spiral staircase leads to Mo Morrow's compact loft office, a space just big enough for one person to work comfortably. On the main floor a majestic stone fireplace is the focal point of the new room; to one side a bank of windows and a window seat invite gazing out over one of the pastures. In the room contemporary seating, neutral colors, and Southwestern accessories keep the feeling streamlined

The old dresser in the bedroom glows with romance. The silver dresser set was a first anniversary gift from Mo Morrow's grandfather to his bride. The crystal lamp and the dusting powder case were hers as well, and she made the lace runner. Carol Morrow added the wallpaper.

Not just symbols of the past, the windmills are still used to pump water into the cattle tanks (TOP).

The patio area is furnished with dozens of colorful tables made of broken and odd tiles. Their bases are old sewing machine legs, which have been painted blue (MIDDLE).

The area of Texas in which the McIntyre-Morrow Ranch is located is Hereford country. This breed of cattle has been raised here almost exclusively for generations (ABOVE).

A dirt road cuts through the valley to the headquarters of the ranch. Oak, cedar, and pecan trees shelter the rock ranch house from the blistering sun.

and relaxed. In this new wing, designed to blend with the main house, the Morrows also included another bathroom, storage, and a screened-in porch, which is home to an inviting hot tub. After a typical dawn-to-dusk ranch day, a soak is a welcome respite.

Although the new wing and kitchen were decorated in a more contemporary style, most of the furnishings in the rest of the house belonged to Mo Morrow's grandparents. Carol Morrow found that she loved the art deco style of the dark wood furniture, the charm of Vivian McIntyre's handmade quilts and tablecloths, and the delicate collection of china and crystal. Paint, wallpaper, and new window treatments were all that were needed in some rooms to make the transition from old to new.

During the cool months of winter, the couple spends a great deal of time outdoors enjoying the grounds, which have not changed much since the time the McIntyres lived there. Much of the whimsical landscape design can be credited to Miguel Duran, the ranch's caretaker since the 1940s. In the backyard several colorful tile-topped tables—Miguel's creations—lend a festive atmosphere to barbecues and outdoor family dinners. Inverted whiskey bottles form decorative borders around backyard pecan trees. Wagon wheels form the front gate. To one side of the house, a refreshing water tank serves the garden and doubles as a swimming hole on hot, dusty days.

The grounds were not created strictly for leisure, however. A mini-farm is subtly incorporated among the swings and lawn areas. The caretaker and his wife tend a garden filled with tomatoes, onions, jalapeños, and more; peach, apple, and apricot trees produce luscious fruit. The pecans are picked and frozen until ready for use. A wall of bamboo protects the garden and orchard from hungry javelinas and deer. The chicken coop provides white, brown, and even blue fresh eggs. Even the peacocks, brought to the ranch by Vivian McIntyre, are not present just for looks. They strut and cry angrily when strangers approach.

Carol, who grew up in urban areas, and Mo Morrow have adjusted easily to the peacefulness of the ranch. Although they continue the family tradition of entertaining at home, they savor their isolation and their outdoor activities, enjoying horseback riding, fishing, and camping on more remote acreage of the property. In the early morning and at sunset, the stillness is magical, broken only by the occasional mournful low of the cattle.

PRAIRIE-INFLUENCED CONTEMPORARY
AN AIRPLANE HOUSE
NORTH OF EL PASO

The organic architecture of the house is evident in the pale native stone of its massive pillars and walls and the strong vertical and horizontal lines of the wood-framed windows. Reflected in the glass is the blue outline of the nearby Organ Mountains (LEFT).

The pitched roof of the house, which encloses 6,400 square feet of space, harmonizes with the surrounding mountain forms. The small gazebo to the left of the house is a peaceful site from which to appreciate the quiet and solitude of the desert (RIGHT).

Since the beginning of the Southwest's written history, the area around El Paso has been a meeting place of cultures and races. The first were the Spanish and the Indians in 1598, when the Spanish explorer Juan de Oñate reached the green valley on the south bank of the Rio Grande, and local Indians showed him and his men through the narrow mountainous route farther north along the Rio Grande.

From that time on, travelers followed Oñate's route, and the green valley became a way station. In 1659 missionaries established a church at what became known as El Paso del Norte. In 1680, when the Pueblo Indians of New Mexico revolted against Spanish rule, some 2,000 Spanish settlers from the north moved south, swelling the population and spawning further growth in the area. By the turn of the eighteenth century, the Spaniards had regained supremacy and people in the Rio Grande communities settled into a pattern of raising cattle and sheep and farming in fields irrigated by water from the big river.

By the early nineteenth century, El Paso del Norte was an

important stop along the trade route between Santa Fe and Chihuahua City, Mexico. Anglos were settling in the area by the 1820s, and when war ignited between the United States and Mexico in 1846, American troops entered El Paso del Norte unopposed. The war ended in 1848 with the Treaty of Guadalupe Hidalgo, which ceded a large portion of the land north of the Rio Grande to the United States. Around the same time, the diverse settlements on the north side of the Rio Grande, directly across the river from Mexico's El Paso del Norte, became the American city of El Paso.

El Paso rapidly became an important frontier city. By 1884 four railroads had entered the city to open it to the outside world, and by the turn of the twentieth century, its population had swelled to 16,000.

As El Paso developed, it followed the path of many Sunbelt cities with inner urban congestion and outer suburban sprawl, leading some residents to the inevitable search for a quieter weekend life. Among them was attorney Malcolm McGregor, who owns an historically important house in El Paso's Sunset Heights district and whose law office is in the heart of downtown El Paso. He felt the need for a change of style and pace from his thirty years of full-time city living.

A man with a passion for aviation, Malcolm McGregor ended his search for a new home site at Cielo Durado ("Golden Sky"), a "fly-in" residential community developed by a group of Continental Airlines pilots in the early 1980s. After a nation-wide search, they had chosen the windswept high desert near the Texas–New Mexico border because of its abundant sunshine, low humidity, and scant rainfall. Ideal flying conditions and the beauty of the Organ Mountains made the pilots' decision easy.

Cielo Durado was developed on what had been a working farm. Utilities were placed underground as a safety measure for the airstrip, and a pleasing result is that the sweeping vistas remain unmarred. On one side of the community, a paved road allows residents to motor their cars up to their back doors; on the other side, a 4,000-foot paved runway al-

Daylight streams through the hangar's windows, illuminating the cobalt blue of the 1936 open-cockpit Stearman trainer and penetrating into the living room's main seating area. The two chairs were made from Gustav Stickley designs; the couch is Victorian. The tongue-in-groove wood ceiling and the hangar's painted steel trusses are visible above the planes. The house, with its heavily insulated roof, air vents at the roofline, and two fireplaces, is remarkably energy-efficient despite its soaring ceiling height.

This bird's-eye view of the open kitchen shows the dramatic natural-wood light fixture above the central island work station. The rock and natural-wood construction of the kitchen is reminiscent of the work of Frank Lloyd Wright, who influenced the architect, David Hilles.

A padded, hand-tooled leather saddle is used as a design element. Maps line the wall. A stuffed rattlesnake sits on a cowhide on the half wall which divides the living area from the airplane hangar (RIGHT).

The curved red oak spiral stairway (RIGHT) was made by hand by two young brothers of the New York Spiral Stair Company of North Vassalboro, Maine. The stairway leads to a loft-study area. Animal hides—and there are many in the house—cover sections of the Arizona flagstone floors, and some are used as throws on sofas, chairs, and beds.

A turn of the century glass-shaded lamp and octagonal table sit near a chair once owned by Henry Trost (MIDDLE RIGHT). The area rug is a replica of an Indian design.

The dining table and Hepplewhite-style chairs, early twentieth-century reproductions that once belonged to the owner's mother-in-law, are placed within the large, open living area. The whimsical biplane wall fixture, which once hung in an El Paso bar, adds to the eclecticism of the house (RIGHT).

lows them to take off for the two-hour, forty-minute flight to Guaymas, Mexico, for a day of tuna fishing.

Most of the homeowners in the community solved the problem of airplane storage by building hangars instead of garages, but Malcolm McGregor has done things a little differently. He has built a unique country house and parked three airplanes in his living room. In addition, he owns a Beechcraft staggar wing, a rare marvel of mechanical design, which reflects the classic period of aviation. Only a connoisseur of airplanes would consider owning one, since replacement parts have to be handcrafted. Aviation buffs consider the "Beech" a work of art.

When Malcolm McGregor decided to build a house at Cielo Durado, he asked a friend of some thirty years' standing, architect David Hilles, to design an "airplane house" where airplanes and people could live side by side. As Hilles put it, "I was given a simple idea but a complex problem." The architect created a design for his client that unifies two almost contradictory structures—house and airplane hangar.

As a first step, Hilles visualized the interior space of the house. He asked himself, "How does one live with air-

planes?" A four-foot drop from an open living room to an enormous space where the gleaming planes sit at the runway level of the house was the architect's answer. He provided, in effect, an airplane "gallery" for a 1936 open cockpit Stearman trainer, a Piper Super Cub, and a Cessna 180. The design makes the planes, along with a colorful engine-driven ultralight hanging from the ceiling's steel trusses, the focal point of the sitting area above. With the flip of a switch, the owner can open the south-facing hangar door, climb into his Stearman, and taxi out to the runway.

Industrial engineering had to be adapted to a human scale in this unusual dwelling. Freespan steel trusses bridge an eighty-foot span. Originally the design called for laminated wood trusses, but the idea was soon scrapped for a more economical and practical solution. The dark painted steel works well with the lightness of the planes themselves. The result is a balance of horizontal and vertical lines allowing for a feeling of unlimited space.

The north side of the flat lot was raised so that the driveway, entry and living room, bedrooms, bathrooms, and open kitchen are four feet above where the planes rest. As a result,

owner and guests can sit in the living room and have clear view of the Franklin Mountains through the high windows of the hangars.

The architectural style of the wood and stone house is reminiscent of the work of Frank Lloyd Wright and of Henry Trost, who had a thriving architectural practice in El Paso from 1909 until the 1930s. Trost, who was the architect of Malcolm McGregor's in-town residence and his law office, was one of the inheritors of Frank Lloyd Wright's legacy of organic architecture and the Prairie-style house, which em-phasized horizontal lines, open interior spaces, and neutral colors. The natural materials of the airplane house—the native stone of the massive, rectangular pillars and square chimneys, and the cedar shake shingles of the hipped roof—are characteristic of organic architecture; the form of the house, along with its materials, fits the environment. The front exterior has strong vertical lines, and the sharply pitched roof repeats the angles of the mountains beyond.

In the interior, in order to carve a more intimate space within the thirty-five-foot-high ceiling, a balcony used as a

A cozy fire blazes in the natural rock-faced fireplace in the library (LEFT). High windows let in diffused light above built-in bookshelves and cabinetry. The chair and the couch are Gustav Stickley designs.

The architect designed several over-sized natural-wood light fixtures for the house (RIGHT). The fixtures had to be large to be in scale with the house's voluminous ceiling, which is thirty-five feet at its apex.

study was designed above the living area. A built-in desk and a personal computer fill a portion of the space, and biographies, historical works, travel narratives, and the twelve volumes of the Oxford English Dictionary reveal the owner's interests. Western bronzes, reproductions of the work of Frederic Remington, are part of the decor. The loft also discreetly offers a door to the utility room, and in one corner of the study is an extra futon, covered with blankets and animal furs.

Because great height explodes from above the low area underneath the balcony, the architect created small vertical spaces with large wood light fixtures in the entryway and kitchen. The wide, open kitchen has a floating chopping-block island that repeats the horizontal line of the light fixture above it, creating an intimate, personal niche in the face of large volumes of space. The kitchen is very contemporary, with state-of-the art cooking appliances, but because it faces the dining area and opens onto mountain views, the space is warm and inviting.

The master suite, which is warmed by a stone fireplace in cool weather, is furnished simply. A white-furred skin is

A multi-colored ultralight dances above three planes—a 1936 open cockpit Stearman trainer, a Piper Super Cub, and a Cessna 180. They are displayed in the stepped-down hangar portion of the house.

Beyond the bright colors of the the stripped ultralight and the cobalt-blue fuselage of the Stearman trainer, structural elements of the house can be seen—the painted steel trusses, the clerestory windows and the loft-study area.

thrown on top of a futon, and the walls are covered in gray wool tweed fabric. The master bath is small but luxurious, with sunken bath and porcelain sink. The guest bedroom, located opposite the master suite, is furnished with a futon covered with a cow's hide and matching cowhide settee.

Throughout the house, Arizona flagstone floors and rough-hewn cedar walls carry out the Southwestern desert design.

In the main living area, which faces the airplane display, are heavy, dark, Shipley-designed chairs and a carved Victorian-era couch. The furnishings, which are simple and eclectic, bring together such whimsy as a small replica of a biplane that is used as a bar in the dining area, a Western saddle, Indian blankets, Brazilian cattle hides, snake skins, and raccoon pelts, and combine them with pieces of classic design, such as the silk-covered Victorian settee and turn-of-the-century Hepplewhite-style dining room chairs. The result is an interesting mix of ideas, periods, and materials that only adds to the enjoyment of this thoroughly masculine house.

Angled behind the living room is a library sitting area where a fireplace soars up to the high ceiling. When lit, its fire throws warmth and light into the living room.

Outside, wood railroad ties, lumber salvaged from a dairy, and heavy timbers from old bridge trusses are used around the exterior and in the simple wood gazebo on the east side of the house, where the owner can sit and hear the wind move across the flat plain and through wind chimes. Here, he can see the quail, roadrunners, and doves that frequent the property, and smell the essence of the Southwest— sage, mesquite, and juniper. Purple verbena and Spanish brooms, whose yellow flowers bloom in spring along with daffodils are judiciously planted among the native desert plants. And if the weather is fine, Malcolm McGregor can roll open the hangar door and explore the countryside by air in the old Stearman.

From the Cielo Durado runway, the sloping roof lines of the main house and the gazebo stand out dramatically against the early morning sky. The clerestory windows on the north and south sides of the house warm it in winter and keep out the hot sun in summer; they also provide daytime lighting and are electrically controlled to ventilate warm air. The Piper Super Cub is parked just outside of the open hangar door which is forty-five feet long and eight feet high, perhaps one of the biggest doors in residential use.

ARIZONA

Beneath a crystalline blue sky, in the unblinking gaze of a fierce sun, Arizona has always been remote and unyielding. From the high plateaus of the north to the hilly grasslands near the Mexican border, the state is now boomingly prosperous.

Behind the shiny newness of recent building there lies a cultural legacy that reaches back thousands of years. Today the best of Arizona's architecture and design has its roots in the past. Arizona's history, imbued with legends and mysteries, has seeped into the bricks and mortar, making what came before inextricable from the present—and future. Traditions die hard here.

Arizona, its name derived from two Indian words meaning "little spring," covers some 114,000 square miles of striking geography. In the north, vast, seemingly endless mesas suddenly fall off into canyons too spectacular for the heart and eye to comprehend in a single glance. Sweeping through the center of the state are cool stretches of pine forests, gentle birch groves, and icy-cold trout streams. In the west and south, the deserts dominate. The Mojave, sneaking across the California and Nevada borders, gives way to the vast Sonoran Desert, which reaches upward from Mexico and encompasses both Tucson and Phoenix. The Sonoran, in turn, pushes up against the Chihuahuan Desert, also shared with Mexico as well as Texas.

These arid lands, lush in their special vegetation and dotted with otherworldly mountains and buttes, color the landscape of Arizona. The harsh conditions have forced its inhabitants to adapt; for man, it has meant creating shelters that work with the environment rather than conquer it.

Archaeologists are not sure when man first appeared in Arizona, but there seems to be evidence that hunters tracked game here as early as 12,000 B.C. Some one thousand years ago, advanced Indian civilizations were establishing complex cities on the barren plateaus of northern Arizona. Using local materials, they chipped out sandstone blocks from the surrounding land and built their multi-family residences. Ruins of such cities can be seen today just outside Flagstaff. Later, in the central portion of the state, large multi-story limestone and mud dwellings were built into the sides of cliffs in the Verde Valley along the Verde River, where the agrarian people could both fish and farm and still have protection from predators. Wooden ladders, probably made from the abundant trees that lined the river, provided access to the cliff dwellings. When enemies approached, the ladders were pulled up.

In the Sonoran and Chihuahuan deserts of the south, the Hohokam, a highly civilized people, settled the area between what are now Tucson and Phoenix. The Hohokam, who built crude homes of mud and brush, were adept at coaxing food from the hard soil. They built a complex series of canals, channeling water from the few rivers in the area to irrigate their crops. In later years their building techniques became more sophisticated; some of their mud structures attained heights of four stories. Wall height was achieved by piling and patting wet mud into place, allowing it to set, then adding more layers in the same manner. Logs were lined up as beams to hold the weight of the upper stories; saguaro cactus ribs and brush were also used to hold the mud in place.

By the time the Spanish arrived in Arizona in the mid-sixteenth century, the Indian culture was strongly established. The Spaniards, conquering Mexico for the crown, pushed northward through Arizona in search of gold and other riches. Not far behind the conquistadors came the Spanish missionaries, who provided a stabilizing element for the European military in a harsh new world and attempted to convert the indigenous peoples. More often than not, the padres were forced to keep the peace (and their lives) by blending traditional Yaqui and other Indian rituals with customary Catholic pageantry, creating a local variation on Catholicism that was compatible with everyone's beliefs. It still exists in one form or another in some parts of the state.

Jesuit missionaries established a series of missions from northwestern Mexico up into the Tucson area. Using unskilled laborers, the padres introduced the use of adobe bricks. The laborers would dig up the earth at the proposed mission site and form the mud into rough rectangles. Most of the first mission buildings were quite plain, although by the onset of the eighteenth century, naive versions of Spanish baroque ornamentation relieved the humble adobe walls. The mission San Xavier del Bac, which still stands near Tucson, was worked on during the 1700s by the local Indians and Mexican artisans.

By the early nineteenth century the Spaniards had lost their zeal for the New World. In 1821 Mexico declared its independence from Spain. After the Mexican War (1846–1848) between Mexico and the United States, the northern portion of Arizona became part of the United States territory; in 1853 the rest of its area was acquired from Mexico through the Gadsden Purchase.

With that, the Anglo settlement of Arizona began. The first English-speaking people were a rugged lot, mostly men, passing through Arizona on their way to California's gold. Once the Anglos decided to stay in the territory to pursue mining, farming, ranching, and other ventures, it was necessary for the U.S. Army to come in and build forts to protect citizens from attacks by Indians, most notably the Apaches.

The architecture of this period, which we now call Territorial, generally followed the earlier building patterns in its use of mud and mud bricks. Protection from the elements and marauders were the first requirements of the Anglo settlers. Like the Mexican settlers before them, the Anglos built crude adobe houses with small windows and doorways.

By the 1880s peace with the Indians had finally been achieved and a brand-new railroad, the Santa Fe, snaked its way through Arizona. For housing, this meant that the architecture could become more open, less fortlike, and use more sophisticated materials. Wood, glass, bricks, and more came via the rail, and with that, the Victorian era reached Arizona. Modest adobe dwellings were gussied up with columns and corbels; residents worked furiously to copy the ornate styles that were the rage in the East. Before long, frame houses appeared in abun-

dance, and the adobe styles were left to the Hispanic population.

The Mexican residents of Arizona maintained the urban architecture of their native country. Entire blocks of flush-front adobe row houses were common in cities like Tucson. To the street these simple houses showed only a narrow doorway and perhaps a small window. Home life was conducted in the rear courtyard. The flooring material was usually packed mud, and canales, or drain spouts, moved rainwater from the flat roofs away from the vulnerable wall material. Rooms were added as families grew.

After Arizona joined the union in 1912, it experienced several decades of steady but gentle growth. Ranching, mining, and farming were major industries. It was soon discovered, however, that the exotic landscape, the Indian population, the dry climate, and the cowboy legends were major attractions for romance-starved Eastern tourists. The Santa Fe Railroad astutely acknowledged this trend and set up a system that could accommodate and capitalize on the thousands of new tourists. The railroad hired architects to build hotels and train stations in styles that fulfilled the Easterners' romantic vision. These new buildings influenced the styles of residential buildings. At the Grand Canyon, one of the Santa Fe Railroad's outposts, architect Mary Colter designed a series of Indian-inspired stone buildings, which set a trend for stone buildings throughout the state. Elsewhere in Arizona, dude ranches, resorts, and winter homes for Easterners sprang up in revived Spanish Colonial, Indian, and Territorial styles.

After World War II, the growth in Arizona—particularly in Tucson and Phoenix—began in earnest. The advent of air-conditioning in the 1950s made 115-degree days more bearable, even comfortable. Industries found the business climate favorable also. Military personnel, stationed or trained in the state, returned after their tours of duty ended to make the desert home.

In this expansive setting, the desert spawned a creative modern architectural environment. While some transplants insisted on bringing environmentally unsuitable housing styles with them, many others were inspired by the desert's savage beauty and sought shapes and materials that complemented the landscape. Frank Lloyd Wright lived and practiced architecture in the desert northeast of Phoenix for several decades. His designs for the region emulate the rugged angles of the surrounding mountains and blend with the land. Taliesin West, his architectural community, still thrives there. Paolo Soleri, an Italian architect who studied briefly with Wright, found his vision transfixed on the future. Arcosanti, his city of tomorrow, is currently being built into the side of a mesa in central Arizona. Unusual shapes and high-density housing will be its hallmarks. Still other architects and designers have chosen to build in a style that echoes the state's early days: handcrafted adobes, whimsical stone cottages, and ornate, Spanish-influenced haciendas.

The growth continues at full speed. Although some of the old adobes and Victorian beauties have been lost to progress, many are being saved and restored. And the new designs—the best of them—acknowledge Arizona's colorful past as well as its future.

VICTORIAN ADOBE

ORNATE SPLENDOR ON TUCSON'S MAIN STREET

T he idea for the founding of Tucson was brought forth on a hot day in August 1775 when a colonel in the Spanish army, Don Hugo Oconor, and one of the greatest missionaries in the history of the Spanish expansion in the New World, Father Francisco Garces, decided that a military outpost was needed along the Santa Cruz River at a small settlement.

The outpost was to be a part of the Spanish system of presidios, or garrisons, of which there were seventeen along a 2,000-mile frontier stretching through what is now Texas, New Mexico, northern Mexico, Arizona, and California. The existence of the presidios served a dual purpose for the Spanish—to protect their interests from marauding Indians and, later, to form the genesis of new communities. The place along the river the men chose had been settled much earlier by ancestors of the local Pima Indians. The name *Tucson* is a Spanish corruption of the Pima word meaning "the place at the foot of the black mountain."

In June of 1777, a new commander, Captain Don Pedro Allande, was assigned to the fledgling presidio. He was a

Once an open carriage house, this structure (LEFT) was long ago enclosed and plumbing and electricity installed to turn it into apartments. Today its rich Southwestern elegance, with the brick-paved portico, traditional roof with vigas, and natural wood posts, is the result of the Tocis' restoration.

Late spring in Tucson allows for the blooming of various petunias, snapdragons, and sweet alyssum in the garden (RIGHT). In early spring, a collection of iris bloom; some of the bulbs are from Patti Toci's grandmother's estate in South Carolina. Nasturtiums, roses, and sorrel are also grown here.

The lush garden was once an asphalt parking area. The contemporary Mexican fountain in the garden is exactly in alignment with the center of the foyer and can be seen when entering the house. The fountain was found in a village deep in the interior of Mexico. It was hauled to Tucson in pieces in a vegetable truck, a process that took seven months.

Late afternoon sunlight casts long shadows through a gate along the wall that separates the garden from Main Street. The interior arches lead into the back courtyard (LEFT).

The table is set for an informal meal in the back veranda room, which was added in the 1940s or 1950s and affords a view of the lovely garden and fountain. The room's quatrefoil-design cement tile adds informality and Southwestern graciousness to the room. An old child's wagon is filled with a collection of duck decoys.

wealthy man, and when Spanish government funds were not available to build fortifications at the renamed San Augustin del Tucson, the money came from Captain Allande. On May Day, 1782, the presidio was attacked by a force of 600 Apaches. The garrison survived, but Captain Allande was convinced that further protection was needed. He pushed for the completion of a three-foot-thick adobe wall ten to twelve feet high to enclose San Augustin del Tucson.

The wall enclosed ten acres of land, and its gate, a massive mesquite door secured by iron bolts, was located where Main and Alameda streets intersect today in the Arizona city of Tucson. El Camino Real (the royal road), the lifeline of the community, ran parallel to the presidio's west wall and stretched all the way south to Mexico City. At the beginning of the nineteenth century, the roadway, which became known as Main Street, was the first street of great economic and social importance to Anglo-American Tucson. As late as 1915, remnants of the presidio's wall were still standing.

By 1826 the first Anglos visited Tucson, which was by then under Mexican rule. By mid-century, with the purchase of almost 30,000 square miles by the United States from Mexico, Tucson became an American town, and its cultural mix of In-

dian, Spanish, Mexican, and Anglo worked to give Tucson its distinct flavor.

The little community slowly opened up to the outside world. Stagecoach lines came into Tucson, among them the remarkable Butterfield Overland Mail, the fastest transportation existing during its time. A passenger could travel from St. Louis to San Francisco in twenty-five grueling days.

In 1880 Tucson had a population of 7,000 people, and on March 20 the Southern Pacific Railroad arrived from Los Angeles, bringing excitement in the town to a crescendo. From that moment forward, people from all parts of the world came to Tucson. Goods previously brought into the territory laboriously and expensively became readily available, including wood, bricks, machine-made furniture, and the Victorian trim so fashionable in the late nineteenth century.

As Tucson began its stretch toward prosperity in the late 1800s, fortune seekers settled in the little community and commerce boomed to meet the demands of the permanently stationed United States military garrison and the ever growing gold- and silver-mining concerns in southern Arizona.

As the standard of living continued to rise, prosperous citizens could afford to take a fresh look at their own dwell-

Lovely white wicker graces the south parlor, where a white lace tablecloth covers a tea table. Most of the pieces were acquired from a Main Street estate. Forty yards of the floral chinoiserie fabric were used for the upholstery in this room. The double French doors lead to the entryway and the north parlor.

ings and alter them far beyond the requirements of the simple, windowless adobe shelters of the early Indian and Spanish settlers.

Some prominent Tucsonans built gracious houses on Main Street. Edward N. Fish was the first to build a grand house, a classic example of the Mexican adobe town house, in 1868. A native of Massachusetts, Fish became a prosperous merchant and owner of the first steam-operated flour mill in the Arizona Territory. His house, located on the southeast corner of Main and Alameda, was on the site of the gate to the old Spanish presidio. With thick adobe walls, ceilings fourteen feet high, and flat roofs, the Mexican adobe town house style included a zaguán, which cut through from the entrance to the back patio, where the cooking took place in traditional Mexican fashion and where the family was likely to sleep during stifling summer nights. In the climate of the Southwest, interior cooking created too much heat, and the danger of fire spreading to other parts of the house was great, so cooking took place either outdoors or in a separate cook house.

The Fish house was fitted with luxuries such as hardwood floors and English Victorian furniture, all made possible after 1880 by the relatively low freight costs of the railroad. The Fish family was soon joined by other prospering families, including that of Hiram Stevens. The Fish and Stevens houses were adjoined, and together the two couples began a tradition of graciousness and hospitality on Main Street; Mrs. Fish even entertained President and Mrs. Rutherford B. Hayes on their tour of the West in the 1880s. The street remains what has been called by Southwestern architectural historian and author Janet Ann Stewart the "architectural and social museum in the heart of downtown Tucson."

Another house on Main Street, in what is now known as El Presidio Historic District on the National Register of Historic Places, has also been an important part of Tucson's history since the end of the last century. Built originally as an unadorned, four-square adobe with a typical flat roof, the house first appears on the Sanborn fire map of 1896. The maps were commissioned by the town of Tucson for insurance purposes, and they have remained as key documents in Tucson's architectural history.

According to Janet Ann Stewart, the house was built in the 1890s, most likely by T.C. Kresham, who had a grain, produce, and fruit store on Congress Street in the 1880s. The

high-ceilinged rooms opened to a twelve-feet-wide zaguán that led to the back garden, as is the case today. Stewart has unearthed evidence that the original adobe dwelling cost 1,200 dollars to build, and the 1889 remodeling took another 1,500 dollars. At some point, Victorian accoutrements—a wide, sweeping veranda and a balustrade, one of the first in Tucson, atop a hipped roof with a vented gable—were added. Decorative brackets adorned the eaves, and slender posts appeared on the veranda. The traditional adobe became a graceful Victorian house in a coupling of eastern and western architectural forms that became known as American Territorial. These houses represent a transitional style, bringing together Mexican, and therefore Spanish, adobe building traditions and American wood and brick construction, along with simplified decorative details borrowed from English Victorian architecture.

This newly restored house is known as the Kruttschnitt house, named for Julius Kruttschnitt, the son of a president of the ever powerful and vital Southern Pacific Railroad and one of Tucson's most important citizens in the early twentieth century. A graduate of Yale University, Kruttschnitt moved with his family into the Main Street house in 1912. He quickly became a pillar of Tucson society while he managed the Southwestern properties of the American Smelting and Refining Company. He was an example of the new breed of well-educated people who came to Tucson after the turn of the century. He and his family lived in the house for almost twenty years.

After the next four decades, when the house changed hands several times, Kruttschnitt would have scarcely recognized his proper Victorian house. In 1979, when Gerald and Patti Toci bought the property, the main house had been subdivided into four apartments. The graceful veranda had been stripped away, and the house was weighted down with two heavy, round, concrete pillars stuck into a concrete stoop serving as a nondescript entryway.

The Tocis' actual involvement with the house began in 1967, when Gerald Toci rented an apartment in what originally had been an open pavilion where carriages were kept behind the main house. The pavilion had been enclosed years earlier and had been broken up into small apartments. Patti Toci came to live there when the couple married in 1969. Although they moved on to live and renovate elsewhere, they retained the cozy Main Street apartment as a Tucson version of a pied-à-terre.

In 1979 the Tocis saw a turn-of-the-century photograph of

New double French doors lead from the house's entryway into the living room (LEFT), which has been used as a dining room and a hallway at various times. The clock against the wall is an English eighteenth-century family heirloom. The English cane-sided oak couch and chairs date from around 1900; between the couch and chairs is a pegged and dovetailed Irish immigrant's trunk. The square vigas in the ceiling, which are no longer structural, are hand-hewn pine from the local Santa Rita Mountains and were original to the house. The Tocis suspect they are older than the house, perhaps having been used from an earlier structure in the time-honored Southwestern tradition of recycling building materials.

In the Tocis' north parlor (ABOVE), the owner's Victorian approach to the house's interior is evident. The lady's writing desk against the north wall was acquired from another Main Street house and is an example of the Eastlake Victorian style. On the floor near the window is a collection of children's Victoriana, including the doll, another Main Street legacy. The restored picture molding visible near the ceiling is original to the house.

the house and became enchanted with the idea of restoring its Victorian splendor. They bought the property, moved back into their old apartment, and began restoration work.

Immediately, they had difficulty finding craftspeople who knew about old adobes or Victorian fretwork and gingerbread. Although Gerald Toci, a Western artist and airline pilot, did the design work and Patti, a caterer, was a "willing laborer," they needed help. Luckily they found Rafael Contreras, a skilled craftsman living in Mexico who knew about rebuilding crumbling adobe walls. Help came, too, from Paul Weiner, an architecture student at the time, and a team of eight other students who managed, in about three months, to refurbish the exterior. They ripped off the 1950s apartments on the north and south sides of the house and stripped off stucco to reveal the underlying adobe. The existing adobe was shored up by wiring and plastering. The students rebuilt the veranda and the balustrade on the roof and installed new electrical and plumbing systems.

Through the original double front doors beneath a rectangular transom, one enters the traditional Southwestern zaguán, a wide center hall, which aids air circulation and provides a central axis from which all rooms emanate. The zaguán concept was critical in the Southwestern climate, where temperatures can zoom to 110 degrees or more in summer. Central air-conditioning was not introduced until decades later. The Tocis use the air-conditioning now installed in the house during the hottest part of summer.

From the foyer, two front parlors, common in Victorian architecture, are found to the left and right. Patti Toci chose to give each one a Victorian ambience. In the north parlor, windowsills reveal twenty-two-inch-thick exterior walls. The beehive fireplace in the corner of the south parlor, so unmistakably Southwestern in style, offers a refreshing juxtaposition to the Victorian white wicker seating areas. The Tocis have played successfully with the blending of Southwestern with eastern American styles, making the home restful, pleasant, and often surprising.

Beyond the parlors, the zaguán forms a central room that has been used over the years as a dining room and simply as a hallway. Now used by the Tocis as a living room, they have

In the master bedroom, collectibles are displayed on top of a late-eighteenth-century blanket chest from Delaware (LEFT AND BELOW). The chest was designed to resemble a chest of drawers rather than a blanket chest; its two top drawers are fake, and the top lifts off. Two hurricane lamps, early-twentieth-century mechanical clocks, old mirrors, dresser scarves with crocheted edges, all set the mood for a past era. The silver-handled brush on the right is inscribed "Christmas 1897." The large oil lamp on the right has been electrified. The painting hung above the blanket chest is signed "J. Goodloe." Gerald Toci's mother painted this scene when she was fourteen years old. Part of an old quilt collection is draped near the closet door. A "Grandmother's Flower Garden" quilt covers the bed.

furnished it with turn-of-the century English oak furniture with caned sides. The Oriental rug was purchased by its original owner from Marshall Field's in 1912, as its label still clearly attests. This room provides one of the house's delightful contrasts. One can sit on the Victorian furniture and yet clearly see the traditions of the Southwest by glancing up at the exposed dark wood vigas set in plaster. The master bedroom with a new bath and a second bedroom are found on either side of the living room.

The back "veranda" room pays tribute to the Tocis' well-thought-out approach to restoration. Although they feel over the years the house was thoroughly "remuddled," they retained certain modifications made by previous owners. They restored the veranda to three sides of the house instead of the original four. The back "veranda" room was designed and built to give the entire rear of the house a courtyard feeling. The room feels entirely original to the house, however—a Victorian solarium of sorts, with a sloped roof and tongue-in-groove ceiling—and provides a transition to a lovely garden courtyard area and a recently installed Mexican carved stone fountain. The·Mexican red, white, and green floral cement tiles covering the floor of the veranda room are from the 1940s or 1950s.

The garden courtyard is a rich tribute to Patti Toci's skill as a gardener. On what was once an unsightly asphalt parking lot there is now a sinuous complex of curved paths constructed with stone pavers and old bricks rescued from a hospital; several large trees including a palm, pine, and mesquite; a collection of iris, Victorian roses, edible herbs, peach and plum trees (prized for fruit in the mid-1800s), and a profusion of well-tended geraniums.

On the north side of the property is a restored stable building, rebuilt as a garage and used as a carpenter's workshop while restoration continues. Along the southern property line is the original carriage house and kitchen, which has been home to the Tocis, off and on, for almost twenty years. The tile-roofed carriage house portal, which has massive peeled pine posts, beams, and rafters, has been restored. Terra-cotta pots of lush greenery line the portico.

After years of planning and backbreaking work, the home is now restored to its American Territorial splendor and has become a jewel in Arizona's architectural heritage.

The Tocis feel they have been amply rewarded, because now they can enjoy using all the structures in the compound as home, just as previous owners did a century ago.

132

The Tocis are collectors of quilts, airplane memorabilia, Indian baskets, tin advertising art, and hurricane lamps from the turn of the century. Part of their collection is on display in the north parlor, in a twenty-two-inch-deep windowsill that reveals the depth of the walls (LEFT).

This cast-iron steeple-point hinge (ABOVE) with ornate scrollwork was typical of the Victorian period. Matching hinges were found throughout the house on original interior doors. When the Tocis discovered a few major openings in the house that once had doors, they restored them to their original lintels and installed French doors. The matching hinges for the replaced doors were found through an antique iron collectors group.

133

The decorative brackets on the veranda were made on site with hand tools. The simple crossed-bar railings and vertical posts are painted stone blue. The fascia atop the ornamental brackets and a band underneath them are painted a rich pumpkin color.

The Toci home on Main Street (RIGHT) is a part of Tucson's architectural heritage. The Victorian, center front gable gives the house a feeling of solid support; the balustrade, or "widow's walk," atop the hipped roof, so fashionable in the late nineteenth century, was one of the first in Tucson. The graceful veranda wraps around three sides of the house and covers 1,300 square feet.

MEXICAN COLONIAL TOWN HOUSE
ARTISTIC RESTORATION IN
TUCSON'S BARRIO HISTORICO

Like so many cities in the Southwest, Tucson has changed dramatically in the forty years since World War II. The Old Pueblo, as the city is affectionately known, once prided itself on its successful mix of cultures. From its earliest days, Tucson has been a racially easygoing city; its old, established "first" families have heavily intermarried. By the 1970s, however, social divisions were drawn more along lines of wealth and property.

In the postwar era, Sunbelt cities experienced unprecedented growth. In the 1950s, Hughes Aircraft moved to Tucson, becoming the city's first major industrial employer. As Davis-Monthan Air Force Base grew, so did its employment of civilian as well as military people. With increased wealth, the population began moving east and north, away from the downtown area where commercial enterprises had flourished. Growth proceeded helter-skelter; Tucson, like its sister Sunbelt cities, had not adopted plans for management of such rapid growth.

By the 1960s, the oldest parts of Tucson, where people of all races once lived in close proximity, were mostly populated

Late afternoon sun enriches the adobe wall on the front of the Larsen house, where a tree casts its shadow near one of two doors which face the street (LEFT).

Matching twenty-four-paned French doors lead into the family's sitting room from the brick-paved outside patio and a wicker seating area (RIGHT). The doors were found in a salvage yard in Tucson called Architectural Antiques. The floral stained-glass inset above the doors was handmade by the owner.

by Hispanics. The barrio, or neighborhood area, was in decay, witnessed by crumbling houses and commercial buildings and gaping vacant lots—all reminders that the energy of the city had moved elsewhere.

When the idea of urban renewal, of rebuilding abandoned downtown areas, swept the United States in the 1960s, the concept hit Tucson with a vengeance. Plans were made to develop a community center and a privately funded commercial hub to draw people and resources back to the center of town.

Completed in 1971, the Tucson Community and Convention Center has been a focal point for activity in the downtown area, and La Placita Village has served its commercial needs. But redevelopment was costly to Tucson's history. Two hundred adobe homes were destroyed for the community center, and others were moved or destroyed for additional urban renewal projects. Fortunately, the zeal for rebuilding the downtown area brought forth renewed interest in the city's physical past. Plans to cut the barrio area in half by a freeway

were scrapped, and in 1974 a municipal ordinance created historic zones where buildings were protected to some degree from demolition. New projects had to pass through an architectural review board before construction could begin.

People whose houses had escaped the wrecker's ball during the height of urban renewal could breathe a sigh of relief. The barrios, in addition to providing a place for people to live, also served to foster a sense of ethnic identity and cultural awareness. One such neighborhood is known as the Barrio Historico, which was made a Tucson historic district in 1975 and was listed on the National Register in 1978. It is also known popularly as Barrio Libre, or the "free zone," and it was here that local Mexican customs and mores were kept free from Anglo influence and laws. Since the mid-1880s, Barrio Libre had been known for the darker side of lawlessness—murders, street brawls, cock fights, and a well-established red-light district.

Despite its turbulent history, there is another side to Barrio Libre. With houses arranged in rows flush to the street, the

A Mexican Cristo in a tinwork frame and an Indian basket sit atop the living room fireplace's narrow mantel (FAR LEFT). The ornate gray fireplace surround may have been part of an old radiator; it was unearthed at a swap meet. While the fireplace was being restored, old wagon wheels that had been used to shore up brickwork were found.

In the living room (LEFT), a pencil cactus frames one side of an arch leading to the dining room. The contemporary bent-willow furniture was purchased in Tucson. The raised-paneled, low-drop-cross shutters, designed and built by Chris Larsen, were inspired by a pre-1900 door he admired. They were heavily varnished to give them a patina of age. The contrasting paint on the lower part of the wall, an example of dado detailing, is characteristic of Mexican interior design. In the ceiling, narrow rectangular boards were created by Chris Larsen as a variation on traditional round vigas.

139

barrio is a highly personalized community where people share yards, resources, and the very streets themselves. The streetscape in the barrios is very much like that found in the Mexican state of Sonora, the ancestral home of many Hispanic Tusconans. The feeling of cooperation is still in evidence today as the neighborhood experiences the changes the 1980s have wrought.

As urban renewal in Tucson cut around the heart of Barrio Historico, the neighborhood became isolated and disconcerted. Young people of all races with strong feelings about Tucson's history began moving in, however, and have infused the area with new vitality. They are people for whom the restoration of historic homes is a passion and a way of life. In the barrio, they share trucks, tools, information on old techniques, and their own labor. It was in this context that Chris Larsen, an artist, and his wife, Sally, a teacher, decided to buy a dilapidated adobe house on Convent Street in Barrio Historico in 1981.

The abandoned, crumbling house became a full-time job for Chris Larsen during the ensuing years of hard work. When he was finished, he had spent three times the money and twice the number of years he had planned in the restoration of the 2,000-square-foot house, but what he accomplished would have pleased Doña Teresa Elías.

Doña Teresa was the widow of a prominent and prosperous Tucson rancher and legislator, Jesús María Elías. The adobe was their town house, bought in the barrio's heyday in 1882. Elías was also, by community standards of the time, a respected Indian fighter. He was involved in what has been judged by later observers to be a dark episode in Tucson's history, the Camp Grant Massacre of 1871. An armed group of 148 men, led by Elías and an Anglo, William Oury, raided Camp Grant, some distance from Tucson, where a group of Apaches lived. The vigilantes suspected the group of a brutal raid in the Santa Cruz Valley, but the eighty-five Apaches who were massacred that morning were women, children, and old

---

The kitchen was built from scratch during the restoration of the house, on the site where an earlier kitchen lay in ruins. The cabinets, once used in an old smoke shop in Tucson, were the basis for the scale of the new kitchen. Mexican marble lines the countertop, and the floor was designed by the owner. He arranged cream and blue Mexican ceramic tiles in a modified square pattern set with diamond shapes and added an elaborate border that only an artist with a keen sense of geometry could have devised. The six-burner commercial gas stove was purchased at a local restaurant supply house. The nine-foot harvest table was made in a Mexican Mennonite colony.

men; the younger men were away from camp, hunting. The men from Tucson were brought to trial for murder, but a jury of their peers found them innocent after nineteen minutes of deliberation.

Jesús María Elías did not build the Convent Street house. The Larsens have traced property records to anonymous owners in 1878; they bought the house from the Mejias family, who had owned it since the 1940s.

It took two and a half years to repair and rebuild the crumbling walls and to put a roof on the adobe ruin in Barrio Historico. Chris Larsen brought a great deal of enthusiasm to the project but quickly learned that Arizona, unlike New Mexico, lacked a thriving community of experts on adobe restoration. Since professionals were hard to find, he read what he could and spent a good deal of time tracking down people who had done adobe work themselves. He was blessed often with the advice of old skilled craftsmen. He learned mostly by trial-and-error, however, and became a good plasterer in the process. Because he worked without a precise plan in mind, Larsen was able to respond freely to the visual demands of the house, much in the same way he, as a painter, responds to a canvas.

His first task was to try to protect the house from its greatest enemy, the weather. During the ten years the house had been abandoned, it had been ravaged by water coming in from a leaky roof. Larsen worked in sections, removing the roof, rebuilding walls, and then constructing a new roof. Fifty percent of the walls were replaced using modern methods to rebuild the adobe. Wall surfaces were covered with one-inch chicken wire and then coated with plaster. Expanded metal lath was nailed to the walls where large-scale cracking was likely, as well as where new walls were joined to old. He also bought forty-pound bricks of adobe stabilized with emulsified asphalt to further aid in water resistance. The new walls were thirteen feet high and fourteen inches thick.

Although square corners and a tin roof were found on the original house, Larsen rounded the corners and created a highly unusual plaster cornice around the top of the roofline. He took his cue from the cornice treatment on an 1874 Tucson house he admired, a style he had also seen in Sonora, Mexico. He thinks that the barrio style that developed in Tucson a

century ago was closely linked to northern Mexico as well as to the city's then prevailing American Territorial style, in which traditional, flat-roofed adobes acquired Victorian trim and gabled roofs.

After some research, he quickly realized that making a plaster "running mold" for a decorative cornice was rarely done. He read what he could about the method, which required using thin plaster and a plasterer's brush to throw it up on its support. The running mold was a mold that was used to cut the plaster into a smooth, continuous line. First, he made the mold, framework, and scaffolding with the help of old books on plastering. By way of the barrio grapevine, he heard of an experienced plasterer, Arnulfo Herreras, who lived only two blocks away. Herreras taught him how to use old tools and apply the plaster properly.

In his approach to materials, Larsen reveals his underlying love for artistry and infinite patience for the restoration process. Items were acquired cheaply, but the amount of time required to comb through demolition yards, junk stores, flea markets, and wrecking sites was exceptional. When he went searching in hardware stores for spare parts for some of his treasures, salespeople were astonished and often told him such parts had not been made for forty years. Larsen was undaunted; he would talk to tinkerers and would create what he needed, such as plumbing parts from an old heating radiator.

Two fine examples of Chris Larsen's sense of objects and sense of space are the house's bathroom and kitchen. The twelve-by-fifteen-foot bathroom is new, make from what might have been a third bedroom or a parlor. It is a just tribute to his artistic sensibility, full of light from a skylight and with enough room for the couple to feel as if they had stumbled on a luxurious bathroom in a prewar London hotel. The top of the wall was torn off, and a new roof, ceiling, and skylight were added. The room's great glory, an enormous solid porcelain tub, dates from about 1906 and was found in a ditch. Gumwood cabinets with enormous mirrors were pieced together from what remained after the kitchen cabinets—originally from a turn-of-the-century smoke shop—were installed. The bathroom doorway was built around an 1860s door found on a construction site.

The kitchen is spacious, visually satisfying, and clearly shows the artist's eye for balance and symmetry. It feels like the heart of the house, a joyous place in which to prepare food or to sit over a beer at the nine-foot harvest table. The space was expanded and rebuilt from the ruin of a poorly

143

The quilt-covered brass bed which is used by the Larsens' young son was pieced together after its component parts were bought at a swap meet. This room and the living room were part of the original 1878 house. The ruddiness of the walls was created when they were first plastered with a cream color; a slip of red-pigmented plaster was then thrown on top and troweled into the wet plaster.

built existing kitchen that had been added to the home around 1925. The kitchen was built to the scale of one fourteen-foot cabinet and three twelve-foot cabinets, all from the old smoke shop. The marble for the countertops was bought for 160 dollars by a friend traveling in northern Mexico.

Chris Larsen's painterly eye is most evident in the remarkably plastered surfaces of the main rooms. With the help of local craftsmen Miguel Quiroz and his son, Larsen plastered the interior rooms in what he calls "three-coat work." First, a scratch coat of high lime cement plaster was applied to the walls of a room and made roughly level by a comb-like implement that was dragged over them. The high lime content allows the walls to breathe so that the adobe underneath, which easily "wicks" up water, has a chance to dry out. The walls were "set up" for a week or two before the brown coat was applied, which brought the walls flush and smooth. They were "floated" with a trowel to make them sandpaper rough. The very thin skim, or finish coat, was applied to give the smooth white or colored finish of interior plaster walls.

In the Larsens' master bedroom, illuminated with a 1920s-era commercial skylight, the finish coat, while still wet, was painted in an inventive palette of color that allows for wonderful play of light. In this room, Larsen was assisted by Chris Estrada, a young man from the neighborhood. Dry pigment colors were broken into a wheelbarrow of wet plaster with a chef's whisk. The colors they used were a brownish eggplant purple, beige, and blue. A wall was divided into roughly five zones; in the top zone, the purplish color alone was worked into the gypsum; in the next zone, the ratio of color was roughly four to one, purple to beige; the third zone was two to two; the fourth, one to two; and the bottom zone was beige only. Patches of blue were cut in at random. The result is a pleasing and restful symphony of color.

The interior walls are all quite different, yet all have an interesting patina because of unusual uses of color. The living room, part of which made up the original 1878 house, was plastered with a contrasting thirty-two-inch border in a traditional Mexican terra-cotta color. The antique quality of the border was the result of the color having been applied over the lighter plaster while it was still wet.

The living room is furnished simply and pleasingly with bent-willow furniture purchased locally. The room has highly polished fir floors and a saguaro-ribbed ceiling with traditional vigas, variations of which were created throughout the

In the sitting room is a white wicker love seat, Indian rugs, and a painting of a beach scene by Chris Larsen.

house. Along a zaguán, or wide hallway, heading east from the north end of the living room, the master bedroom, bathroom, sitting room, and dining room project from either side.

Recently Chris Larsen built a studio in back of the house. The 1,000-square-foot structure has interesting old doors and a working neon sign from a demolished Tucson movie theater glowing inside. It is his place to begin painting again now that the house and the studio project have come to an end.

Artists have been attracted to the barrio for some time. Upon reflection, Chris Larsen thinks the area attracts a certain kind of character which he admits includes anyone like himself who would would spend years restoring an old house. "People who are willing to piece together an old house themselves are in some way unusual. One way this strangeness

exhibits itself is in arguments about which technique is the right one. One of my neighbors was trying to brick his driveway in a herringbone pattern while neighbors looked on and shook their heads sadly. We are all extremely independent."

It is estimated that about 60 percent of Barrio Historico's buildings have undergone some degree of restoration. The neighborhood continues to change and will do so as long as it is alive. Today old houses are being bought and restored by people who can afford contractors and who might not live in the houses themselves. The eventual owners of these houses will have a different view of the neighborhood from people like the Larsens and the Hispanics who have lived there for generations. The spirit of the barrio is likely to make them good neighbors too.

The bathroom reflects the crisp, clear design style of the 1920s. The enormous ceramic tub, found abandoned in a ditch, is so heavy that it took six people, a lift-gate truck, and metal pipes for rolling to get the tub into the house. The black and white rectangular tiles form a pattern the owner has liked ever since he saw it in the Paris subway. The green-tiled accent on the floor was made from a box of one-inch hexagon tiles.

The Larsens' master bedroom walls are a tribute to the artist's plastering vision (LEFT). With a young man from the neighborhood and wheelbarrows full of color and plaster, Chris Larsen has created a large canvas of color that changes as light streams into the room from the overhead skylight. A family quilt is on the bed, and above the simple wood-framed fireplace is one of his early paintings. Through the bedroom door is the sitting room; beyond the French doors, the back patio.

STONE COTTAGE

A RUSTIC RETREAT IN THE FOOTHILLS OF THE CATALINA MOUNTAINS

Built in the early 1940s, this stone house (LEFT) emanates a rustic charm. To build the two-story structure, river rocks were hauled from a nearby wash and set in mortar with the help of a two-by-four framework on the inside of the structure. Each foot of wall height was allowed to harden slowly, to prevent the weight of the rocks from collapsing the wall. Recent additions are the redwood decking on the roof and the ramada, or shade structure, which creates an outdoor "room." The beams of the ramada are old telephone poles made of fir, which were found on nearby Mount Lemmon.

French doors lead from a deck surrounding the new wing into the master bedroom (RIGHT). The leaded glass window was salvaged from an old house in Chicago.

For more than forty years, the road up to the stone house in the foothills of the Catalina Mountains north of Tucson was not much more than a wide desert path that cut back and forth between the mesquite trees and underbrush. Used by the occasional truck, car, or horseback rider, the road was tooth-rattling at best. Twice a year, the residents of the house, along with their neighbors, would get out their shovels and haul trailers of sand to repair the damage done by winter rains and car tires.

Although the ownership of this two-story desert dwelling changed several times over the decades, its residents all bore a common trait. They were hardy individualists, preferring to contend with the forces of nature rather than the confines of civilization. The house was set on a pristine piece of the desert, elevated above the city limits; on a good day, it was said, one could almost see to Mexico. For those who lived in this house only about twenty miles from Tucson's center, life was serene and simple.

The history of the house is loosely linked with that of three other stone houses situated further uphill. In the early

1930s, Randolph Jenks came to Tucson from New Jersey to study at the University of Arizona. Being short on resources but long on energy, Jenks was able to build himself a modest adobe house with the help of a fellow student and an elderly Yaqui man. From that adobe, which was also located in the Catalina foothills, Jenks homesteaded more than 600 acres, including some land around nearby Bird Canyon. It was there that he chose to build a split-rock house for his family and two smaller stone houses for ranch hands and guests. He found a source of water high up in the mountains and built a pipeline system down to his property so that he could raise cattle.

Besides adobe, stone has always been a common building material in the Southwest. Its use in housing is so ubiquitous that its history is somewhat difficult to determine. As long as 900 years ago, the Sinagua Indians built elaborate dwellings at what is now Wupatki National Monument in northern Arizona utilizing sandstone slabs stripped from the area's geological formations. Some 300 years later, they traveled into central Arizona and built protected stone and mortar dwellings into the sides of cliffs. Early settlers of the area scoured riverbeds for rocks they could use to build shelters against the broiling heat. The thick stone and mortar walls with small window openings provided a reasonable temperature within. By the early 1900s, Indian Revival was the prevailing style in national park lodges, due in part to the savvy marketing of the Santa Fe Railroad system, which gave eastern tourists a romanticized vision of the West. Architect Mary Colter built Hopi-inspired stone buildings at the Grand Canyon around the turn of the century; her designs in turn engendered the building of rustic rock guest ranches, lodges, and homes throughout the state. In the late 1930s and 1940s, Frank Lloyd Wright, who started Taliesin West, an archi-

---

Agave, barrel cactus, prickly pear, and ocotillo frame the flagstone walkway to the front of the house (RIGHT).

The Bernsteins built a patio (TOP RIGHT) between the main house and the guest casita, using brick pavers. The patio is home to a collection of cacti and succulents. Occasionally a javelina or two will make a guest appearance on the patio.

The roof deck (BOTTOM RIGHT), which has spectacular views of the nearby city, is the locale for casual dining. The table settings are from Mexico, as is the pitcher. The wildflowers were gathered from the nearby desert.

The new wing, containing the master bedroom and bath, was built to blend with the original house. The rooms were actually built on top of a hill that abutted the back of the old house. Because there was no access for vehicles to the top of the hill, all of the stones (found in nearby washes), buckets of mortar, and other building materials had to be hauled up to the construction site by hand.

A terra-cotta beverage pot (LEFT) was made by the Tarahumara Indians of northern Mexico.

The tub in the new bathroom (RIGHT) is clad in Italian tile. The mullioned windows, salvaged from an old Tucson home, provide vistas of the hillside and of the javelina path, which winds down toward the patio and kitchen door.

tectural community outside Phoenix, used desert rock and mortar as the primary building materials for the community's buildings. It was his philosophy that the native rock helped to blend the architecture with the surrounding landscape.

Jenks may or may not have been influenced by this trend, but he did note that rocks were plentiful on his land, and during the Depression, building materials were not so easy to come by. He gave his houses a touch of sophistication , however, by cleaving the rocks in half and using the smooth, flat sides on the exterior walls.

In 1944 Jenks sold the houses to Major Lenox Lohr, president of Chicago's Museum of Science and Industry, who used the ranch as his winter retreat, then moved his ranching operation to its present site on the Arizona-New Mexico border. Jenks also owned a parcel of land downhill from his homesite. For several winters, he had allowed a retired Ohio contractor and his wife to park their trailer on the property. The couple, Arthur and Tacy Binns, admired the restful landscape and the expansive views. When they decided they wanted a permanent place to spend their retirement years, Jenks sold them the land.

The Binns, who were Quakers, quickly began building a two-story, stepped-back house, also using rock and mortar construction. Rather than cleaving the stones in half, however, they retained the natural jagged and rounded forms of the rocks on the exterior walls. With the help of their son and some Mexican laborers, they hauled stones from the nearby canyons and dry washes and pieced together the simple house, which hugs a low hill. The exterior walls are battered back; they are thicker at the bottom to support the weight of the materials. Inside, the walls are plumb. To set the walls, the Binns used two-by-four slat forms on the interior, and built the walls slowly, foot by foot, so that the mortar would harden properly and hold the weight of the rocks. The average thick-

Hooked on the wrought-iron banister of the living room staircase (LEFT) is part of a collection of jute shigra bags, used in Ecuador for carrying food, seeds, or other necessities. The tapestry on the wall is a wool shawl from Bolivia, probably dating to the 1920s. The ceremonial mask is from Peru, made of tropical bird feathers; the nose is a corncob. The knotty pine paneling is original.

ness is eighteen inches, which insulates the house from the fierce summer sun almost as well as adobe.

To build the chimney for the living room fireplace, the Binns set up a wooden frame and placed stones around it. Once the mortar set, the inside frame was burned out. The big, cheery fireplace was used to warm the house on cool evenings, although there also was a heater for particularly cold winter nights.

Downstairs, a kitchen, dining, and living room took up most of the floor space; upstairs, there were two small bedrooms and a bath. Just outside the driveway, the Binns added

In the living room (LEFT), a mixture of traditional Midwestern antiques and primitive arts and artifacts is set off by the large, cheery fireplace. A ceremonial hand-held mask from the Tapirape tribe of the Amazon region is displayed above the fireplace; its tropical bird feathers are held in place with beeswax. The figurines on the mantel are pre-Columbian, probably from Mexico. The split-rattan basket comes from the Philippine highlands. The Victorian secretary is made of cherry and walnut.

The guest casita (ABOVE), added after the original house was built, was used primarily as a storage room. The Bernsteins finished the interior, adding Mexican tile flooring and a hearth and mantel to the fireplace. Today it serves as guest quarters and home office. The oak bed is a Midwestern antique; the tapestry above the bed is a ceremonial piece from Peru. At the foot of the bed, a brewing pot used by the Shipibo Indians of the Peruvian Amazon sits on a kilim rug from Afghanistan. On the hearth, the wood and cloth puppet is from Indonesia.

a special touch: a water spigot for thirsty hikers and horses, surrounded by a low rock wall and capped by a quotation from Isaiah: "Ho every one that thirsteth come ye to the waters," which still greets parched visitors. The Binns' house reflected their simple religious philosophy; nothing was for show, all was functional. Nonetheless, the house had undeniable organic charm.

The Binns lived there for about ten years, enjoying the remote setting and the many long walks they took in the desert hills and canyons. They contended with the inevitable washed-out road and water pipelines broken from mountain rockslides. They were always ready to fix things themselves. Eventually, ill health forced them to sell their home and move into town.

The house has had a succession of owners and tenants, all connected by the adventure of rural living and the need to escape the growing urbanization of Tucson. Author Edward Abbey, a self-proclaimed desert rat, resided there, as did a naturalist/ecologist. Up the hill, the Lohr estate was also home to some interesting individuals: a famous pop singer's daughter, a follower of a Muslim mystic, a doctor who spurned traditional medicine in favor of botanical cures.

In 1980 Jeanne and Michael Bernstein bought the old Binns house. Like their neighbors up the hill and the house's previous residents, they possessed adventurous spirits and uncommon occupations. Michael Bernstein, a primitive arts dealer, specializes in pre-Columbian artifacts and Amazon tribal crafts. His wife, a former antiques dealer from Chicago, helps with his business. After traipsing through the jungles of Ecuador and exploring the Philippine highlands, they found the stone house to be a quiet getaway, a calm home base for them and their young daughter.

The house and the guest casita, which was added after the Binns moved, were in reasonably good shape. Only a small amount of cleanup was necessary to make the dwelling livable, even though the couple knew there were changes they wanted to make to the house. They approached remodeling with care, not wanting any new structures to appear tacked on to the original construction. With the help of two local stonemasons, Michael Bernstein learned rock work. They added a simple garage to the back of the guest cottage and a low fence around the perimeter of the two-acre property. "It was hard work," the owner concedes. "We gathered rock from washes and from our land, matched the mortar to the original, and fitted each rock—like a mosaic—to make straight walls. I learned to appreciate stone masonry as an art form." A brick patio was tucked in between the main house and the guest casita, and a ramada, or shade structure, and redwood decking were installed on the roof over the living room, making the rooftop usable space for outdoor living.

For their needs, the Bernsteins found the main house too small, so they chose to add a new master suite to the back of the second story, placing the addition on top of the abutting hill. They jackhammered through the back wall of the second floor to connect the old with the new, and picked and jackhammered the footings for the new wing into the hill. A redwood deck with stairs leading back down to the patio was added outside the master suite.

Attention was then turned to the interiors of the main house and casita. In the guest house, Mexican tile flooring was installed over the unfinished concrete slab surface and the walls and ceiling were redone. The structure, which also doubles as an office, has a small stone fireplace and is decorated with a mixture of primitive art pieces and Midwestern antiques.

The original knotty pine paneling in the main house was

A stonemason built the bedroom fireplace freehand without the benefit of a firebox or liner. The feathered pieces on the wall behind the fireplace are ceremonial headdresses from the Xingu Indians of Brazil; the large pot at right is a brewing container for a kind of beer made by the Shipibo Indians of the Peruvian Amazon. The broom and basketry are from the Philippines, and the pottery on the mantel was made by Ecuadorian Indians.

cleaned and oiled to a soft sheen and the linoleum flooring replaced with Mexican tile. The decor is a blending of primitive and traditional pieces, favorite items culled from years of traveling and buying. Upstairs, the former master bedroom provides extra space for guests. The new wing, although hardly discernible on the exterior from the original structure, contains the creature comforts of the 1980s. A cozy fireplace warms up the bedroom, and in the bath, corner windows surrounding the sunken tub reveal the spectacular scenery.

Wildlife continues to wander the foothills. Several generations of javelina, wild and distant relatives of the pig, make regular evening visits, grunting down a path that swings by the bathroom window, in search of victuals. Normally shy creatures, this javelina family was somewhat tamed by the previous residents of the house. Other visitors include coyotes, mule deer, skunks, quail, snakes, an occasional bobcat, and a ringtail cat who makes his home in the garage.

Unfortunately, urban growth is creeping up on the charming stone house in the foothills. New houses are being built close by, and the old dirt road has been closed off. Today access to the stone houses is through an electronic gate and up an asphalt road. Although these modern-day conveniences have taken a bit of the romance away from the area, the Bernsteins have adjusted. For them, their quaint stone abode is still their solitude.

The arched entrance of the roof deck leads to an exterior staircase. The curved stonework frames desert, mountains, and Tucson beyond.

Ancient saguaro cacti rise from the desert floor near the stone house. These cacti, native to the Sonoran Desert in Arizona and northern Mexico, also manage to grow on the rocky slopes of the nearby Catalina Mountains (LEFT).

From the roof deck, spectacular sunsets and dawns create a vivid panorama (FAR LEFT).

CONTEMPORARY PUEBLO STYLE

A HANDCRAFTED ADOBE IN
THE TANQUE VERDE VALLEY

Palo verde trees line the hand-cobbled driveway to the Butlers' handcrafted Pueblo-style adobe near Tucson's Rincon Mountains (LEFT). The owner, a builder, made the adobe bricks for the home on-site, utilizing some 2.5 million pounds of dirt excavated from a nearby wash. The stepped-back architectural design, with its rounded corners and protruding vigas, is patterned after the ancient Indian pueblos of New Mexico and Arizona. The wagon wheel is an antique from Mexico.

An old ox cart from Mexico, filled with potted flowers, welcomes visitors along the front driveway (RIGHT).

Just to the east of Tucson, toward the Rincon Mountains, lies the Tanque Verde Valley, a desert greenbelt. This long swath of oasis follows the banks of the Tanque Verde River bed, forested with shady cottonwood trees, desert willow, and mesquite. It is an area where grassy fields soften the desert landscape and wild birds find sanctuary. Despite Tucson's growth in the last several decades, this valley has remained "the country"; working cattle ranches, parklands, dude ranches, and an occasional golf course take up the majority of the acreage.

Despite its sparse populace, the valley has had its share of history. The Spaniards, during their push northward from Mexico, discovered the river and gave it its name. Apparently they must have seen it during its rainier days, when the water flowed into deep *tanques verde*, green pools or "tanks." These days, it takes quite a bit of rain to fill the usually dry bed.

The Anglos made their first tentative toeholds in the area during the mid-1800s, when small cattle ranching and farming concerns began. At about the same time, the Butterfield

A heated spa is just steps away from the guest house (ABOVE), which is situated at one side of the courtyard. Built into the flagstone patio, a narrow stream trickles down into a fish pond which is filled with goldfish, mosquito fish, catfish, and water lilies.

A local craftsperson made this iron light fixture (RIGHT), with a lizard motif, which illuminates the way to the front gate.

Overland main line, pulled by mule teams, ran a regular stagecoach through the valley, carrying mail and nervous passengers from St. Louis to San Francisco. The passengers and the local ranchers had plenty to be nervous about; this was marauding Apache country, and the Indians utilized the greenbelt as a passageway from the surrounding mountains into Tucson, to raid settlements. By the late 1870s, the army had established Fort Lowell in Tucson for protection, and the Anglo and Mexican ranchers began to prosper peacefully.

The Tanque Verde Valley also flourished. Water was relatively abundant, and Tucson was close by for commerce and supplies. More settlers came. In the 1920s, a prestigious college preparatory, the Evans Ranch Boys School, made its headquarters in the valley, and young scions of wealthy Eastern dynasties were sent there to learn Latin and horsemanship. The school, which remained open until World War II, had a polo field, and among its graduates were such names as Roosevelt, Pulitzer, Vanderbilt, and DuPont. Today the school is a country club, but many of the cattle ranches still exist.

It was in this valley that Laurie and Mark Butler grew up. She was raised on one of the cattle ranches; he was a neigh-

bor who rode horses with her during grade school. As they went through school, they shod horses, entered junior rodeos, practiced roping, and enjoyed ranch life together. It seems fitting that they married. It also seems natural that they chose to build their first home themselves as Mark is a builder and designer.

For their home they had a parcel of land up the road from the old Evans School. Dense with mesquite and palo verde trees, the ten-acre lot is bordered by the Agua Caliente wash, a creek that runs most of the year; a county park; and undeveloped Forest Service land. The Butlers knew that the land would remain remote—at least during their lifetime.

With the help of another local designer, Mark Butler drew up the plans for a main house and guest quarters, to be done in a Pueblo style. Although the thick, rounded walls, protruding beams, and flat roofs of this type of architecture are associated with the Pueblo Indians of New Mexico, historically this kind of shelter also existed in Arizona. The design was therefore appropriate to the site and to the arid climate of southern Arizona.

In keeping with the Pueblo style of the design, adobe was chosen as the building material. "I love the feeling of adobe,"

The curving breakfast bay (ABOVE) has deep-set windows that frame views of the back courtyard and the mountains beyond. The blue color of the window casings is traditional in Pueblo designs; the Indians believed it kept evil spirits away. The trees by the breakfast wing are poplars.

A portal (LEFT) shades a passageway from the kitchen to the master suite. For the passageway, unsealed Saltillo tile from Mexico was used underfoot; the decking material is flagstone from Ash Fork, in northern Arizona. Pots of annuals and succulents add color and interest. The simple bench is a Mennonite piece from a colony in northern Mexico. The hanging gourds were used by Mexican Indians to carry water.

163

A contemporary Southwestern wool rug is a welcoming accent in the entryway (ABOVE). The owner built and designed the front doors and the built-in mesquite desk. The leaded-glass windows were created by a Tucson craftsperson; the ceramic sconces were made by a California potter.

A handmade ladder leads up to the loft that divides the master suite's atrium from the sitting area (RIGHT). The white flooring in the atrium beyond is painted adobe pavers. The atrium houses a collection of parrots.

A handcrafted pine door (FAR RIGHT) leads to a home office. The hand-forged hardware was found during a trip to Vermont before the Butlers started building their house. The small table is from a Mennonite colony in northern Mexico; the pot is made by Tarahumara Indians, also from northern Mexico.

A Koshari (LEFT) represents the clown of Hopi ceremonies. During the ceremonies, the Koshari provides comic relief, as well as teaches a small lesson. This doll version, with its large green melon, warns against the evils of gluttony.

The living room is a mixture of Southwestern and traditional furnishings. In the room, wing chairs blend harmoniously with Mexican pigskin furniture and Mexican ranch antiques. In the hallway, an antique mesquite sugarcane press from Mexico finds a home under a painting. On the living room wall, above the handcrafted buffet, hangs a Navajo rug in the classic Two Gray Hills style. The flooring in the living room and throughout most of the house is oiled and sealed Saltillo tile from Mexico. The overscale hand-carved corbels add weight to the eighteen-foot ceiling.

Mark Butler says. "As a kid, when I shod horses during the summer, many of the ranches I worked on had barns made of adobe. I always remember how cool they felt inside." Although he had worked with the material before, their house was to be his first major adobe project.

A pressed-block adobe machine, a device that forms mud bricks with great pressure, was used to make the adobe blocks. Luckily, dirt found on the property was the right mixture for making the blocks. The first load was made from the earth excavated for the backyard swimming pool, but it was hardly enough. For the 6,000-square-foot main house and 1,600-square-foot guest abode, it was necessary to dig in the nearby wash (fill dirt was later brought in to cover that excavation). In all, some 55,000 adobe blocks were made on-site.

The walls were not the only things crafted on the property. Most of the house's architectural details were either made by Mark Butler or supervised on-site. Cured spruce beams for the ceilings were adzed by hand in his workshop. Mesquite wood cabinetry, flooring, window casings, gates, and doors came out of the workshop. Built-in furnishings—desks, shelves, cupboards—and some free-standing mesquite pieces were produced as well. Even the stones in the long curving driveway were hand set.

In the building, energy efficiency was also a consideration. The thirty-inch-thick walls are good insulators, so there was little reason to add air-conditioning. Instead, ceiling fans and a water-based evaporative cooling system, were installed which keep things comfortable even when the desert temperatures creep over 100 degrees. Where there are larger expanses of windows, shady portals deflect the sun's rays; other windows were kept small.

About eighteen months after they first broke ground, the sounds of hammering, sawing, and drilling ceased, and the three-bedroom main house was completed. The owners

moved in, gladly relinquishing the workshop/apartment, where they had lived temporarily, to its transformation into the caretaker's quarters.

The house, despite its ample square footage, is surprisingly intimate, due in large part to the Butlers' many personal touches. The central living room, with its eighteen-foot-high ceiling and expansive windows, is open, formal. Off to one side, a step up leads to a conversation alcove, where a fireplace (one of six in the house) and bancos, or built-in benches, create a cozy setting. In the library, an overgrown window seat lavished with pillows doubles as an extra bed when the guest house is overflowing. The expansive kitchen, with its mesquite wood cabinets and pantry, has a breakfast bay punctuated by narrow windows, which juts out into the backyard.

The master suite, at the opposite end of the house, also has some whimsical touches. Entry to the wing is via an adobe-paved atrium, which is home to a half-dozen colorful, loquacious parrots. A small loft, which can be reached only by a ladder, separates the atrium from the suite's sitting area and provides a good hiding spot for reading or listening to music. A simple sleeping area, with its own raised fireplace, and a generous bath complete the wing.

The Butlers were of like minds about the furnishings for the house. In addition to the many built-ins and other hand-crafted items, they used Mexican antiques, Mexican pigskin furniture, Navajo and Southwestern textiles, and crafts by local artisans to complement the Pueblo tradition of the architecture. In the living room, however, a pastel dhurrie area rug and several traditional pieces, such as wing chairs, were used to emphasize the formality of the space and to break up the neutral colors found in many of the other furnishings.

The house and the adjacent guest house both open onto

For the bedroom, saguaro rib shutters were created, using the lightweight but sturdy inner skeleton of the tall saguaro cactus. The shutters provide privacy while allowing a bit of light to filter in (TOP LEFT).

The raised fireplace in the kitchen is one of six in the house (BOTTOM LEFT). It usually provides all the warmth that is needed on chilly winter mornings.

Just off the living room, a conversation alcove is an inviting spot on a crisp night (LEFT). Cushions can be used to soften the bancos, or built-in benches. The wool rug is a contemporary Mexican textile; the cheese table, which was carved from one piece of wood, is about seventy-five years old and is also from Mexico.

Overscale handcarved corbels and deep-set window reveals exemplify the Pueblo-style characteristics of the house (ABOVE).

The comfortable breakfast bay (LEFT) affords a view of the back courtyard and neighboring mountains. The table is mesquite, with a Saltillo tile mopboard. Southwestern-patterned fabric on the cushions gives the area an accent of color. The ceiling fan is one of many in the house. The fans provide ample breezes most of the year; in the dead of summer, an evaporative cooler is turned on.

a back courtyard, which was landscaped to resemble a high desert canyon such as those found in the surrounding mountains. A free-form pool with a boulder as its diving board, a heated spa, and a stream that trickles down into a small fish pond were plastered in a mottled blue-black, to emulate the canyon waterways. A ramada, or shade structure, shelters barbecue equipment at one end of the courtyard. To keep with the mountainous theme, the plantings in the courtyard are lusher than those of the surrounding desert, creating the feel of an oasis. Queen palms and poplars provide shade; purple verbena, alyssum, strawberries, and rosemary spill across boulders and hug the edges of the stream and pond. Pots hold colorful annuals. Also in the landscape are old metates and manos, stone implements used by Indians to grind corn, which Laurie Butler found on the ranch where she grew up.

Their natural landscaping efforts have seemingly fooled the locals. A black racer snake drinks often from the pool; mule deer bed down regularly next to the guest house. Quail and other birds come to the kitchen door expectantly, where birdseed has been strewn.

The Butlers' house has worked well with their lifestyle. Even though they both have business commitments in town, they prefer spending their spare moments enjoying the solitude of the country. Friends gather often, staying for informal dinners or barbecues. On weekends, Mark Butler and a group of running companions are likely to dash through the desert to the waterfalls in the mountains, then back again for a swim and brunch. Most of the time, however, the Butlers simply enjoy the quiet of their remote adobe house.

In the kitchen (LEFT), mesquite wood cabinetry and appliance panels were all handcrafted by the owner. The flooring is also mesquite, oiled to withstand wear. The counter tile is Talavera, from Mexico. The plastered alcove ceiling gives the space architectural interest. The antique table and utensils in the foreground are from Mexico; the table is sabino wood. Graphic area rugs are part of a Navajo rug collection.

171

SCULPTED ADOBE

A SPANISH OASIS IN THE HIGH DESERT NORTH OF PHOENIX

The area of north Scottsdale, Arizona, known as Pinnacle Peak takes its name from a mountain with a pinnacle-shaped boulder formation. The peak stands apart from the rugged McDowell Mountains, which punctuate this Upper Sonoran Desert landscape. The high desert is home to palo verde and ironwood trees and saguaro, cholla, and prickly pear cacti. Filling the landscape are creosote, brittle bush, jojoba, and bursage—ubiquitous high desert shrubs. The elevation here is about 2,000 feet, and the cleaner, cooler air makes the climate more agreeable than elsewhere in Scottsdale or nearby Phoenix.

Annexed to the city of Scottsdale in 1982, Pinnacle Peak was only recently rescued from relative inaccessibility by newly paved roads. At the turn of the century, its early homesteaders were hardy cattle and sheep ranchers who settled on large tracts of desert. The ranches remained until the 1960s, when the Valley of the Sun, as the general Phoenix area is known, began its expansive growth. Nevertheless, small ranching operations could still be found in the rocky desert well into the 1980s.

The afternoon brings magical light to the high desert, where artist William Tull has created a unique oasis that, in this view (LEFT), reflects the soft curved lines of traditional Pueblo adobe architecture.

Petunias, which bloom in winter and early spring, add a jolt of color to the high desert near Phoenix (RIGHT).

In the early 1970s, the thrust toward residential real estate development in Pinnacle Peak began in earnest. Changes have been incremental, but the area is rapidly attracting more and more people in search of the quiet desert life.

Pinnacle Peak developers took early steps to ensure that new homes would be well integrated into the desert environment. Due to the scarcity of water, green lawns are forbidden, and most subdivisions have been limited to one-story houses. Some developments have outlawed red-tiled roofs and large, nonindigenous trees; one even requires submission of scale models to an architectural review board. In the opinion of some, the north Scottsdale area, including Pinnacle Peak, will be a development representative of the way Arizona was meant to be—without the regional designs of the Midwest, East, or Far West superimposed on the desert. Pinnacle Peak is coming of age in a style appropriate to its environment.

The pristine desert, good climate, wonderful views of the McDowell mountains, and an integrated architectural landscape have attracted new residents, including a Phoenix restaurateur born and bred in Malgrat de Mar, a small village near Barcelona, Spain. He knew that the one-and-a-half acre site he found in Pinnacle Peak would be the perfect setting for

A jewel-like leaded-glass window with Art Deco overtones shines in the pool pavilion (LEFT).

A gently arched opening leads into the entrada, or entry—a protected flagstone courtyard draped with a delicate willow tree (ABOVE).

One of the forty olive trees which are planted on the property (LEFT). Together the trees produce about 1,000 pounds of olives in a given year; they are then harvested and preserved in five-gallon jars by the owner's industrious parents.

For the interior of the guest house (BELOW), rough-hewn pine furniture and neutral fabrics were chosen to contrast with a bright purple cotton rug. Beneath the window on the right, is a banco, or built-in sitting area, a signature of the house's designer. The Spanish crucifix over the traditional fireplace has been in the family for generations.

The sculpted adobe guest house (LEFT) was designed around an antique wooden New Mexican door purchased in Santa Fe. The small house contains an open living and sleeping area as well as a compact but well-appointed kitchen.

a gracious villa and asked artist William Tull to design a contemporary adobe house that would fulfill his desire. Tull is primarily a painter and sculptor, and his designs for adobe homes are prized in the Scottsdale area. He works each plane of a house as if it were a sculptural composition, and the result are houses that are also pieces of art.

Although the house has elements of the traditional Pueblo adobe style, with its soft, rounded forms, it has been "exploded and opened up," in Tull's words, into a flowing, contemporary environment. In a departure from the traditional adobe, the designer kept the use of wood to a minimum; lines and spaces curve, implying a delicate balance between planning and improvisation. Characteristics of the architecture of Santa Fe, Barcelona, Marrakesh, and Scottsdale are evident in the 7,000-square-foot house.

Serving as general contractor, the owner supervised the year-long building of the house. He and a handful of friends, using an adobe machine on-site, made the 200,000 adobe bricks for the large house, guest house, and two other structures. The twelve-by-sixteen-inch bricks are four inches deep and weigh fifty pounds each. The skill of the volunteer adobe brigade grew as the work went on, but it was a formidable task.

Originally the owner, believing in natural ventilation, considered building the house without air-conditioning, but modern practicality led to the installation of air-conditioning and heating systems. All ductwork was kept underground, however, and passive cooling and heating methods were used. During the warmer months, fans force cold air upward from the floor. In winter, nine chimeneas, or small fireplaces, located throughout the four structures provide warmth and coziness. And the living room and master suite in the main house face true south-southeast, the ideal location for passive solar heating.

Open wooden shutters allow the late afternoon sun to stream across the Mexican dining room table that sits just off the kitchen. The table is set with cobalt blue linen to complement pottery dishes from Tlaquepaque in Mexico.

A Moorish arch leads from the living room (FAR LEFT) into the interior entryway. Sectional couches are enlivened with seafoam-green and sand-colored cushions. The hand-woven rug is Mexican. The large pot was made by the Tarahumara Indians of northern Mexico.

Mirror, vase, and torchiere reflect the Art Deco undertones chosen for the house's interiors (LEFT).

In the guest bathroom (TOP), a handmade ceramic bowl with lion-headed faucet is set within shiny, deep-brown Italian tiles.

A treasured mortar and pestle (ABOVE), originally from Spain, has been used by the owner's family for more than 200 years.

179

Besides heat and cold, another environmental contingency had to be provided for. Rain can be merciless when it splashes on the unyielding desert floor, so an arroyo, or stream, lined with carefully pieced stones, was built around the property to carry away the water that the dry desert earth cannot absorb.

Life seems protected here. An undulating, low adobe wall surrounds the property, and inside the driveway entrance, sixteen carefully tended citrus trees, with neat trenches spaded around each for irrigation, stand guard. Evidence of the sun-soaked Southwestern style of living is clear. An oversized tennis court and pavilion face the home's entry; tall French doors let desert light into the living room and master suite, and the flagstone patio leads to a tiled Jacuzzi, swimming pool, guest house, and enclosed ramada. Views of the McDowell Mountains to the northeast seem to be everywhere.

An old, tattered gate from Santa Fe separates the pool and grassy yard and leads to a secret in the heart of the compound, a meticulously cared-for vegetable garden. The gardener is the owner's father, who spends six months each year living in the guest house with his wife, a superb cook.

The father has managed to turn the flat desert land, once home to only a few palo verde trees, into a horticulturist's paradise. Forty olive trees (which in one recent year produced 1,000 pounds of olives), palms, and a eucalpytus are interspersed with apricot, plum, pomegranate, fig, nectarine, and peach trees. The seeds for tomatoes, lettuce, escarole, and lima beans sprouting in the sun were brought from Spain. A vineyard thrives along the tennis court wall facing the citrus grove, and native desert cacti are present in abundance. A graceful willow embraces the front entryway.

The house was designed to meet specific needs. Just off the gracious living room, with its large French windows, a charming alcove was designed with built-in banco, or bench, seating, a chimenea, a window that can be shuttered against

The sculpted headboard in the master bedroom (FAR LEFT) was designed by William Tull. A dhurrie rug from India, an antique armoire, and baskets from Africa are visual proof that the blending of diverse cultures works particularly well in an adobe setting.

Brought from Spain, this holy figure and its wooden gothic niche has been in the family for generations (LEFT).

A Tarahumara Indian pot rests next to a painted animal skull (ABOVE) which was a gift to the owner by a Taos Indian family.

181

the heat of day, and an artfully hidden television concealed in its own architectural niche. Small areas are tucked in throughout the house, reflecting the private nature of its owner and the designer's belief in the need for cozy spaces to contrast with wider, more expansive areas.

In the interior entry, the openness of the house becomes evident. No interior doors were used in this section; the rooms flow from one to the other, so there is a clear view into the kitchen, as well as the living room and beyond, to the flagstone patio outdoors. The simple, white interior walls give the house a feeling of peacefulness and provide strong contrast for the furniture and objects within.

The interiors were planned with the help of the owner's long-time friend and companion, Elisa Green. Over the years they have collected contemporary and antique Spanish and Mexican furniture pieces and pottery and art from Mexico, Spain, and the American Southwest. They also keep a sharp eye out for architectural remnants, especially doors. The bar adjacent to the living room is made from an old Mexican door, and other old doors have been used in the house's interior and exterior. Since not everything in their collection fits, they have vowed to design their next house around them.

Elisa Green's approach to designing the interior was simple. She used neutral desert colors splashed with brighter hues such as seafoam green and teal. The house is filled with baskets, Indian pots, rugs from Mexico, and medium-scale sofas and chairs in white or off-white, which balance larger, darker pieces of furniture. Her low-keyed approach is evident in a built-in banco where lush, fat pillows are covered in fresh, white duck fabric hand-painted with simple, stylized fern leaves. In each room, pieces the couple brought to the house are mixed with new decorative touches that allow the pieces to shine in the adobe environment.

As the interior of the house settles and gains a patina of use and age, and the outdoor plantings grow larger and lusher, the home is changing and adapting to new ideas. The pool pavilion is being revamped and enclosed. It will house a steam room, startling lapis-colored tile in the bath, and a jewel-like, wonderfully uneven, small stained-glass window designed by a local artisan. A special room for the owner's mother to use as a weaving studio is planned. For lively variation, the owner will make other changes. In two or three years, the gray-green exterior, always responding to the play of light, will be changed to a favored "Marrakesh red." Then the villa will play with the desert light in an entirely new way.

The raised-paneled wooden door from New Mexico (ABOVE) is one of many that have been collected over the years and used throughout the property.

The asphalt tennis court (RIGHT) is 65 by 138 feet, longer and wider than most; the adobe wall surrounding the court was designed so that when balls hit its surface, they do not bounce out.

A pink, luminescent sunset lingers over the side of the house and the landscaped enclosure. Patio furniture, a jacuzzi and a pool ramada ring the poolside.

184

STONE, COPPER AND GLASS CONTEMPORARY
ASYMMETRICAL GEOMETRY IN CAVE CREEK

At the base of the property in Cave Creek, on the sandy banks of Fleming Spring, the foundation and partial walls of a one-room miner's cabin are half obscured by dense desert vegetation. Built of rock in the 1930s, the crude dwelling may once have sheltered a Depression-era miner trying to eke out a living on what was left of the mighty mineral—gold—in the mountains and streams of this community north of Phoenix.

Half a century later, another house was built on that sloping site. Like the humble miner's abode, it, too, was built of stone. This new house, though, goes beyond use as a mere shelter—it is a rugged piece of sculpture cascading down the ridge, a celebration of natural materials.

The owners, Fred and Cathie Rosenbaum, purchased the ten-acre property several years ago when they wanted to move out of urban Phoenix to a remoter part of the surrounding desert. They and their teenaged son Brian, were drawn to the small town of Cave Creek, located about an hour's drive from downtown Phoenix, by its clean air, cactus forests, and rugged terrain.

The house (LEFT) cascades southward down a ridge, facing vistas of Phoenix to the south. Made of native stone, wood, and metal, the house blends into the colors of the surrounding desert scape. Various levels of decks offer the family different areas for outdoor living.

From across the breakfast table, it is apparent what convinced the owners to build on the ridge. The city of Phoenix stretches out on the horizon just beyond the hills (RIGHT).

The dramatic angles of the front entrance create a sense of anticipation, importance. The trellised canopy, lit at night with small bulbs, adds scale. The roof and upper gables are copper, a metal native to Arizona.

The pool (LEFT), situated on a stone platform above the desert floor, was one of the first things to be completed. Cedar decking, which stays cool even under an unyielding sun, surrounds it. Properly treated with an oil based finish, the wooden decks can last for years even in the arid desert climate.

Shaded by an overhang, an upper deck overlooks the desert (FAR LEFT). The stones used for the house were the tailings from a nearby gold mine. The stonemason used a blind-mortar technique to make the rocks appear as though they are simply set on one another. For the corners, he searched through the pile of rocks, finding stones with perfect angles. Few were chiseled into shape. The mason worked for a year putting the jigsaw walls of the house together. More than 200 tons of stone were used.

The town's aura of history and its present-day Wild West ambience added to its appeal. The area was put on the map in the 1870s as a watering spot for military wagon trains traveling between Fort McDowell, outside present-day Phoenix, and Fort Whipple, in the north central portion of the state. About the same time, cattle and sheep ranchers vied for the good rangeland. The sheepherders of northern Arizona found Cave Creek to be the perfect winter grazing land for their flocks, and during the late nineteenth century, there were several sheep-shearing stations in the community. Prospectors came also, when it was discovered that the granite of the hills and mountains yielded gold and, later, gypsum. The min-

The house is situated in a forest of saguaro cacti. Of the numerous stately cacti on the property, only four had to be moved during construction. Native to the Sonoran Desert of northern Mexico and Arizona, the cactus can live for more than a hundred years. A slow grower, it only sprouts "arms" at about age fifty.

On a deck near the dining room (LEFT), a driftwood carving and tableware bearing a Southwestern motif lend a cheerful note.

ing boom more or less ran out not long after the turn of the century, and Cave Creek's growth spurt stopped, at least temporarily. The area continued to be frequented by Apaches from the nearby McDowell Mountains, who came to harvest the fruit of the saguaro cactus and the heads of mescal, from which they made an alcoholic beverage. By the 1920s, Phoe-

nicians found Cave Creek to be a cool weekend retreat, and relaxed with picnics under the cottonwoods, enjoying the small streams and natural pools that were filled with water most of the year.

The community still has a relaxed, weekend quality, and perhaps because of that, the Rosenbaums took their time de-

A three-inch-wide skylight at the ridge of the roof shoots a dramatic shaft of light across the entry and living room. Lined with brass, the skylight also is fitted with small bulbs, so the effect is equally dramatic at night. Cabinetry to the right holds entertainment equipment.

ciding what kind of house they wanted here. They spent time acquainting themselves with the topography of their land, observing that the spring-fed creek flowed almost seven months out of the year (a rarity in the desert) and that local wild animals frequently stopped there to drink. They counted scores of stately saguaro cacti standing sentinel on their property, and on one visit discovered the remains of the miner's cabin, which they decided to leave in its natural state.

By the time they were ready to build, the couple knew what they wanted: a stone house that "flowed" down the south-facing ridge of their land, capturing views of the valley and Phoenix beyond. They also knew who they wanted to do the design.

The architect, William Bruder, who is based in New River, also north of Phoenix, has made his mark in contemporary Southwestern architecture by designing buildings that relate to the surrounding environment. Although his designs are

markedly individual, he has been influenced by such architectural minds as Paolo Soleri, with whom he studied, and Frank Lloyd Wright, who spent many winters at Taliesin West, his architectural community in nearby Scottsdale.

When architect and clients first met, there was an instant connection, and before long a design and floor plan were worked out. The three-bedroom house would have its main entry at the top of the ridge; the lower level would actually snuggle into the partially excavated hill, creating a partial berm house. The palette of materials would be native stone, metal, and wood, giving the appearance that the house was a natural part of the desert scape. The style would be elegant, strong—yet suited to the family's informal lifestyle. And because the Rosenbaums wanted to be fully involved in the construction of their house, they opted to become general contractors on the project.

Not long into the construction, however, tragedy struck.

From the entry, a stairway (LEFT) leads down to the lower, earth-integrated level of the house. Berber carpeting on the stairs softens steps and muffles noise.

The overscale front door (ABOVE) was designed by the architect. Rather than opening on hinges, it pivots. The hallway rug was also his design. Over the entryway, north-facing clerestory windows frame mountain views and, when opened, vent warm air that rises from the lower levels of the house. The trellised canopy theme is extended from the exterior into the house, creating a compact and human-scale entry.

193

Fred Rosenbaum, an avid sportsman, was involved in a serious motorcycle accident and was not expected to live. As her husband hovered between life and death, Cathie Rosenbaum was urged by many to stop construction of the house. But she was determined. "I felt as though abandoning the house would be like admitting he was going to die," she recalls. For weeks on end, she supervised the building from his hospital bedside, never giving up hope. By the time he did recover, the house was moving toward completion.

First to be finished was the swimming pool, built on a raised stone platform projecting from the lower level of the house. Fred Rosenbaum used the pool for therapy, both physical and mental, as he was able to be on the site and watch the progress while he exercised. The massive, multi-level stone walls went up not long thereafter, artistically pieced together by an expert stonemason. Prior to his accident, Fred Rosenbaum had found the rust-colored stone while he was out driving on back roads. Quarried from the tailings of a defunct gold mine, the rocks were the same hues as the surrounding mountains. During the building, strict construction boundaries were established so that little of the natural vegetation was disturbed. Only four or five of the saguaros had to be moved to make way for the house. Two years from the start, the Rosenbaums' retreat was completed.

The approach to the house is up a winding dirt road, from which the southern exposure of the house first becomes apparent. With its multi-level wooden decks, protective overhangs, and miles of vista-capturing windows, the design is powerful, yet blends discreetly with the earth. From the driveway and the main entry on the north side of the structure, the 4,000-square-foot house appears to be one level and rather compact, tucked into the natural desert landscape. This side is solid, protective. Few windows in the angular geometry of the architecture allow visitors to guess what lies within.

A six-by-seven-foot red birch door is the main entry to the house. Rather than opening conventionally on hinges, the door pivots open, giving the entrance a sense of grandeur. Outside, next to the door, a brass wall angles outward, a sleek foil to the rough texture of the adjoining stone walls. Inside, the brass module houses a powder room. From the foyer, the eye is drawn across the main room of the house toward the magnificent views, a dramatic "gift" to all who enter the house. Large banks of windows frame and organize the outlying scenery and draw visitors into the main section of the house, which contains the living and dining rooms set

A half wall hugs the open, raised kitchen (LEFT), separating it from the rest of the main room. Two sinks, butcher block countertops, and task lighting hidden behind brass valances above the counters make the kitchen efficient and easy to maintain. On the left, the "picture frame" windows in the dining room are visible. Set low in the wall, the small openings are designed to be at the eye level of diners seated around the adjacent table.

The breakfast table (ABOVE), with its trapezoidal, sand-blasted glass top, was designed by the architect. Set on exposed aggregate legs, its shape echoes the geometry of the house. The light fixture is a family heirloom. The low wall separating the breakfast area from the raised kitchen actually contains blind storage; dishes, table linens, and even a bar are discreetly tucked behind red birch and alder cabinets.

From the dining room toward the rest of the main room, a sense of the house's volume can be appreciated. Weathered steel and brass-plated trusses float the roof over the rock walls and add to the interior's sense of drama. The ceiling is fir, the flooring is white oak. At the far end of the room, a glass screen tops a partial wall, separating the main room from the master suite.

around an open kitchen. In this large space, white oak flooring adds warmth underfoot; above, structural trusses float the roof over the rock walls, giving a sense of volume. The master bedroom is separated from the living room by a partial wall topped by a glazed glass partition, ensuring privacy while retaining the openness throughout the main level. In the bedroom is wool Berber carpeting, and in the adjacent bath, gray tile is both practical and handsome. The bath, which has its own deck, features a step-down shower and a soaking tub big enough for two.

Downstairs, a family room doubles as a guest suite, and a small kitchen serves the lower deck and pool. Brian Rosenbaum's bedroom is also there, tucked away at the end of a short hallway for privacy.

Throughout the house, the architect's many thoughtful and special touches are evident. In the bathrooms, he contrasted hand-thrown pottery basins with sleek, Scandinavian-designed faucets. Red birch and alder cabinets, crafted to his exacting standards, hold a multitude of family treasures and necessities. Brass-faced fireplaces in the living room and master bedroom become focal points when darkness blankets the exterior scenery. The angular geometry of the floor

In the master bathroom (ABOVE), a hand-thrown pottery basin and a contrasting sleek brass faucet are set in a granite countertop. The window on the right overlooks a private deck.

An Italian granite table and a contemporary brass light fixture, both the architect's original designs, create the focal point of the dining room (ABOVE). The cabinets to the left are also topped with the same green-hued granite. The stone, which was precut in Italy, was six inches too short for the countertop. The problem was solved by inserting a brass-clad heating element into the counter, which keeps foods warm between the kitchen and the table.

plan allowed storage areas to be cleverly integrated into available corners, leaving wide sweeps of space for living. The picture-frame windows were designed to be at the eye level of people seated in the dining room; the same window design was used for the step-down shower as well. And the garage entrance was placed just off the foyer, allowing the Rosenbaums the same pleasure of entering their house as their guests who come in through the pivoting front door.

Light is also an important element in the house. In the powder room, a narrow strip of glass wedged between the brass and rock walls casts light on the rugged surface of the interior stone wall. Elsewhere, sunlight is kinetic, directing shadows and patterns everywhere. A three-inch-wide skylight cuts open the ridge of the entire north-south roofline, beaming a playful line of light into the foyer and living room. Most of the built-in lighting is on touch-sensitive dimmers, allowing moods to be set in the evenings. Lighting under the fireplace hearths makes them appear to float when the rooms are darkened.

Some basics of natural energy have also been put to use. During the winter months, the low sun warms the interiors; in the summer, overhangs deflect the blazing heat. Doors and windows can be opened to inviting breezes, and hot air can be drawn out through gable vents on the north wall.

Indirectly, Will Bruder also had an impact on the Rosenbaum's choice of furnishings. Prior to construction, they had amassed a sizable collection of antique pieces. Once they moved in, they discovered that the ornate furniture could not

hold its own with the scale of the house and the elemental rock, wood, and metal textures. Because there were so many built-ins, they needed only a few contemporary pieces to replace the antiques. Soft, buff-colored leather seating was used in the living room. In the breakfast area is an angular, etched-glass tabletop designed by the architect; in the dining room, the dramatic granite table was designed by him as well.

For the Rosenbaums, Will Bruder's impact on their lifestyle has been nothing short of positive. "This house is not about fads or 'isms,'" says the architect. "I'd like to think it is timeless—an honest expression of natural and man-made materials that responds to the Rosenbaums' needs." The house works well for the family, making it easy to entertain friends who come up from the city, as well as take advantage of the landscape that surrounds them.

By night, the wood, metal, and stone of the living room bask in a warm light (LEFT). A brass-clad hearth and mantelpiece seem to float above the living room floor when lit from below. The chairs and sofa are soft, buff-colored leather. The area rug, an original design by the architect, echoes the theme of the hallway rug. Windows unencumbered by curtains or blinds offer spectacular views of lingering sunsets. When lit, the ridge skylight adds sparkle to the ceiling.

The full drama of the architectural design of the house comes into play at nightfall (ABOVE).

CALIFORNIA

n sixteenth-century Spain romantic novels, filled with tales of chivalry and derring-do, were all the rage. One such book, *Las Sergas de Esplandian*, contained a prophetic passage about a mythical land: ". . . west of the Indies, but to the east of Eden, lies California, an island peopled by a swarthy, robust, passionate race of women living manless like Amazons. Their island, the most rugged in the world, abounds in gold . . ." No doubt the Spanish conquistadors, exploring the Southwest in the name of the crown, were familiar with this book and its references to the legendary island. When they first set foot on a desolate piece of land along the Pacific, they called it California, in honor of the magical isle.

Although hardly an island, this state has proved to be magical for many. Angling along the ocean, California has a landscape that ranges from lush, rain-misted redwood forests to deserts scarcely fit for man or beast. In between, there are snow-capped mountain ranges, verdant valleys, and balmy coastal zones. California's beautiful geography has invited seekers of the good life for many generations.

Long before the Spaniards named the region, various Indian tribes populated it, probably having come southward via the Bering strait and west from the deserts of Arizona. Little remains of their civilizations prior to the Spanish settlements, but it is known that for the most part the tribes were migratory. In the cooler, rainier areas of northern California, the ancient people hunted in the bountiful forests and built crude, conical-shaped huts reminiscent of those found in Siberia. The dwellings were reasonably weather tight; made of boards fashioned from fallen logs, they were built over excavated pits for extra insulation. In the warmer central coast and deserts, the native shelters tended to be even more transitory, constructed of light reed frames and covered in brush. In the summer months those living in the deserts dug into the earth in search of coolness.

When Juan Rodríguez Cabrillo made the first known landing in California, the Spanish explorer found half-naked natives living together in small, temporary settlements. The year was 1542. Looking for the elusive Strait of Anian, thought to link the Pacific with the Atlantic, numerous Spanish explorers followed, sailing up and down the coast of California. It was not until the 1760s, however, that actual settlement began. Threatened by English and Russian encroachment in the north, Spain took a practical tack to securing its North American empire. Soldiers, carpenters, ranchers, and missionaries were sent to convert the local tribes and reap what fruit the land bore for the crown.

Arriving on muleback from Baja California, Father Junípero Serra, a Franciscan, came to what is now San Diego to establish the first mission in the state. In 1769 Serra founded San Diego de Alcala mission near the mouth of the San Diego River. In all, Serra established nine of California's twenty-one missions, which stretch from San Diego northward to Sonoma, the last mission, built in 1823. Connecting the missions was El Camino Real, the king's highway, a roadway that today still runs the length of most of the state.

California's missions took many forms, but all utilized locally available materials and emulated—naively—the churches of Spain. For the most part the missions, built of adobe, were compounds and had wings forming a protective quadrangle. The church or chapel, which anchored one corner, was often built with an imposing espadana, or decorative false front, that made the structure appear bigger to the outside world. Daily life went on in the enclosed patio. The surrounding wings housed separate men's and women's quarters, storerooms, workshops, and tanneries. There were only one or two doors or gates to the outside, which were locked at night for protection. Often these gates and doors were elaborately carved and decorated, again emulating churches of the Old World. Along the inner walls of the patio, a shaded corredor was the exterior hallway between rooms. Just outside the mission compound, the Indians' crude dwellings could be found, along with gardens and a cemetery. A large bell, mounted on the walls of the mission, called workers in from the fields.

In 1822 Mexico declared its independence from Spain and claimed California as part of its territory. Not long thereafter, mission lands were taken away and divided up among favored ranchers. The "Californios" existence at that time, however, was far from idyllic. True, there were fiestas and bullfights, but for the most part, living was tough. Ranch headquarters were squalid at best: dirt floors, hides for doors, a pallet for sleeping, no furniture to speak of.

American settlers began to drift into California not long after Mexico's independence, bringing with them a few building styles that could be copied with the limited materials available. Using adobe as the primary material, some of these settlers built one- and two-story houses (with redwood frames supporting the second story), surrounded by broad verandas on both floors and topped by hipped, shingled roofs.

In 1848 California became part of the United States as a result of the Mexican War. That same year gold was discovered at Sutter's Mill near Coloma, in the north, and the population boom began. As a result, California's statehood was barreled through in 1850, without the usual territorial process.

The first miners were a rough and ready lot, and their houses reflected their personalities. Some dwellings were little more than hovels, tents constructed of old clothes and scrap wood. Entire towns went up in weeks, often held together with baling wire. Fires were frequent. Eventually, however, gold brought not only opulence verging on vulgarity but prosperity as well. The arrival of the railroad enabled the newly rich of California to build stately houses, most of frame construction, which they copied out of magazines and picture books. In the late 1800s these "Victorian" houses became extremely elaborate, embellished with frills and curlicues carved by itinerant carpenters who moved from town to town, plying their trade.

By the late 1800s, other styles were beginning to creep into California's architecture. There was less relying on pattern books, more adapting and creating of a West Coast vernacular. The shingle style, so

popular in the East and Midwest, and a fascination with things Oriental influenced the work of the brothers Charles and Henry Green. Their designs for redwood bungalows borrowed from Indian traditions in houses, which featured raised foundations, wide verandas, and maximum cross-ventilation. Also popular throughout the state was the craftsman style, which featured lavish use of wood in the architecture and hand-crafted furnishings. By the early 1900s San Diego architect Irving Gill began escaping the yoke of tacked-on ornamentation and started designing pared-down houses done in brick, concrete, and stucco.

In 1915 the Panama Pacific Exposition in San Diego's Balboa Park was a watershed event for the state's architectural styles. Architect Bertram Goodhue traveled extensively throughout Mexico prior to the exposition and for the event was commissioned to design a large group of buildings housing exhibits and events. He did so in a Spanish colonial style—red tiled roofs, stucco walls, arched colonnades—and the Spanish Colonial Revival craze swept the state.

By the 1920s show business—and more wealth—migrated to California. Whatever money could buy—a French chateau, an old English hunting lodge—could be built. The search for the good life was also in full swing. Swimming pools were de rigueur in many houses. Large patios, vast expanses of windows, and sliding glass doors gave homeowners access to the balmy outdoors.

This influx of people to the state also brought with it a tolerance—and appreciation—for the new, the experimental, and the downright crazy. It is doubtful that Grauman's Chinese Theatre or the Tail O' The Pup hot dog stand, both Los Angeles classics, could have been built anywhere else. Extremes notwithstanding, modern masters have practiced here, including Frank Lloyd Wright, who designed several Mayan-influenced buildings. Richard Neutra and R. M. Schindler came from Europe and introduced the clean lines of the International Style; in San Diego, Cliff May refined the low-profile ranchos of the Spanish settlers and gave the world the California ranch-style house, of which millions were built for housing-hungry GIs after World War II. In the 1960s architect Charles Moore spearheaded the development of Sea Ranch near San Francisco, wood-clad condominiums that made the most of the spectacular site and gave rise to a contemporary California vernacular.

Today in California the new and the experimental are still nurtured. Originals, such as Frank Gehry, with his angles, colors, and ornamental chain-link fencing, are applauded. The past is also lovingly maintained. The state is golden yet.

SPANISH COLONIAL REVIVAL
GRACEFUL RESTORATION IN
RANCHO SANTA FE

The Spanish Colonial Revival house in Rancho Santa Fe (LEFT) was built during the 1920s. Set on a lushly landscaped hilltop, the house has a 1930s addition designed by noted southern California architect Lilian Rice. The front patio was added to create a focal point for the entry. Bricks from Tecate, Mexico, were used for the low patio walls and planters because their orange hue was more in keeping with the color of the clay tile roof than American-fired bricks.

A wrought-iron outdoor light fixture (RIGHT) was forged onsite during the 1920s construction. The smooth white stucco is typical of Spanish Colonial Revival architecture.

Some five miles inland from the Pacific Ocean, just north of San Diego, lies the elegant and leisurely community of Rancho Santa Fe. Shaded by tall eucalyptus trees, the rambling houses of the village reign over large expanses of manicured lawns and neat rows of citrus trees. Curving roads meander past golf courses and riding arenas, where equestrians practice their form. Over the years, Rancho Santa Fe has evolved into the kind of place where people know one another on a first-name basis, where many families have resided for generations.

It was this relaxed ambience that attracted Jeffere and Marcia Van Liew and their two children to Rancho Santa Fe in the early 1970s. The community attracted them, as did a gracious, Spanish Colonial Revival house they found there. Set in a grove of sycamores and Brazilian pepper trees and ringed by citrus trees, the house is not far from the Pacific. For Jeffere Van Liew, a real estate investor, it was love at first sight. Although he grew up on the East Coast, the Rancho Santa Fe setting evoked memories of his childhood. Within hours, Rancho del Oso, a hilltop estate dating to the 1920s, was theirs.

A small pond (ABOVE) tucked between the den and the living room is rimmed in needlepoint ivy and native rocks, which were unearthed from the surrounding citrus orchards. The pond's lead fixture, "Piping Boy," was cast by Kenneth Lynch of Wilton, Connecticut. The large vine against the living room wall is a pittosporum tobira; willowy papyrus grows out of the pond.

A brilliantly colored bougainvillea snakes its way along the eaves of the kitchen roof (RIGHT). The cupola vents hot air from the attic. It is thought that the long-wearing red-clay roof tiles—original to the house—were made by Mexican workers in California. Lichen gives the tiles a mottled appearance on the north-facing portions of the roof. When a small section of the roof was repaired several years ago, figures were found on the old tiles, such as a stick person and a fish, that had been doodled long ago onto the wet clay.

The front patio (FAR RIGHT), situated between the dining room and kitchen, is also the site of informal entertaining. The tile is from Tecate, Mexico; the handwoven place mats were bought during a trip to Michoacán, Mexico. The pottery is French. In the back corner, cacti and succulents reach for the sky.

After the Van Liews moved in, they chose to move slowly on making any changes or additions to the home. Determined to maintain its 1920s flavor and charm, the family decided to take a few years to adjust to the house and the area. In the meantime, Marcia Van Liew became active in Rancho Santa Fe civic affairs and diligently researched the history of the community and the house.

The small village had been founded in the early 1900s by the Santa Fe Railroad Company, whose executives hoped the hilly land would be the right setting in which to grow eucalpytus trees. It was thought that the trees, which grow as much as ten to fifteen feet in one year, would provide the firm with cost-efficient railroad ties, and more than three million seedlings were planted. The plan was ill-advised. Too late, the company discovered that the wood from the graceful,

aromatic trees was too soft to hold spikes and found itself saddled with a 10,000-acre forest.

The railroad was a very progressive firm for its time, however, and was not down for long. In 1922 the company went into real estate development to recoup its losses from the forestry folly. Its development arm upgraded the acreage by planting avocado, citrus, and English walnut trees and subdivided the land into what were known as "gentleman's ranchos." They added winding streets and a charming village center and, with superb marketing skill, pitched this early planned community to winter-weary Eastern executives, doctors, and lawyers and the Hollywood community looking for a refuge from the excesses of Tinseltown. At one time or another, Howard Hughes, Douglas Fairbanks, Mary Pickford, and Bing Crosby came to reside under the eucalyptus and

enjoyed the area's deliciously Mediterranean, temperate climate.

More than just developing the acreage, however, the Santa Fe Railroad was also instrumental in setting the architectural style for the community. Many of its rail stations and hotels throughout the Southwest were built in what became known as the Mission style of architecture. Inspired by the Spanish Colonial missions of the Southwest, the style began flourishing in southern California in the 1890s and featured elaborate parapets and arcades, belltowers, red tile roofs with wide overhanging eaves, and smooth stucco walls. By the 1920s, due to the publicity surrounding San Diego's Pan-ama-California Exposition of 1915, the Mission style had evolved into a broader architectural context—one which drew from a wide variety of Spanish buildings (not just the

In the dining room (LEFT), an antique French refectory table and Welsh Windsor chairs set the stage for more formal dinners. The antique chairs came in a set of seventeen, including a highchair. Simple matchstick blinds cover French doors that lead to the front patio and walkway.

An antique French bonnettiére, once used for storing fashionable hats, was transformed into a descreet bar in one corner of the living room (ABOVE). The large pots were used by Tarahumara Indians of northern Mexico for brewing their potent beverage, tesquino. The planter above the bar is an antique Mexican tinaja, or tub. The wrought-iron sconces were forged on-site.

missions) and more closely imitated Spanish style and decoration. The red tile roofs were usually multi-leveled with little or no overhang; often buildings were designed around lush patios or courtyards and exterior colonnades served as open hallways. This refined style, known as Spanish Colonial Revival, is what the Santa Fe Railroad chose as the vernacular for Rancho Santa Fe.

In a trail-blazing step, the railroad company appointed Lilian Rice, of Requa and Jackson, a San Diego architectural firm, to be project architect for Rancho Santa Fe; she was one of only a few registered female architects in California during the 1920s. She designed the community center, and inn, and a considerable number of houses in the Spanish Colonial Revival style. As a member of the board that approved all architectural plans for the development, she, more than anyone else, set the tone for Rancho Santa Fe.

In 1928 a Santa Barbara businessman named Glenn Tomlinson was attracted to the well-planned community. Purchasing fifteen hilltop acres, Tomlinson hired architect Handy Wass, also from Santa Barbara, to design a family home. Wass's Spanish Colonial Revival design was approved by Rice and other members of Rancho Santa Fe's architectural review board.

The Tomlinson house, of frame and stucco construction topped with a red tile roof, was designed to angle around a welcoming front garden, a modern derivation of Spanish design, in which the garden or courtyard is enclosed by the wings of the structure. The entry leads to a massive living room with high beamed ceilings and a stately fireplace; adjacent to it is the formal dining room, with French doors that lead back out to the front garden. Tucked in between is a comfortable den. To one side of the living and dining rooms is the kitchen; to the other are the bedrooms. For the bedroom wing, an interior corridor connecting the rooms was avoided. Instead, each bedroom has doors opening onto a covered colonnade that runs the length of the house; moving from room to room required stepping out and enjoying the weather.

The architect specified hardwood flooring throughout the house and had a blacksmith on-site forging the hardware. The wrought-iron gates, sconces, curtain rods, door pulls, hinges—everything—were created on the premise.

As the house was being finished, lemon and Valencia orange trees were planted on the property's hillsides. A large swimming pool was dug into the backyard, from which bathers could see a slice of the Pacific through the hills, and a

Los Angeles-based interior designer Waldo Fernandez set a comfortable yet dramatic tone in the Van Liews' living room that was in scale with the room's generous proportions. The upholstered seating and white floor lamp are his own designs; the coffee table is an old worktable that the designer had cut down. The window treatments, hung on wrought-iron curtain rods are simple cotton draperies, left full and billowy. Extra lighting was added to the beams.

A corner fireplace in the den (ABOVE) is home to whimsical, colorful carvings by Manuel Jimenez of Oaxaca, Mexico. Patterned tile decorates the fireplace. The polychrome pot on the bookshelf is pre-Columbian, from the Casas Grandes Indians of Mexico. The rocker is a family heirloom.

Meant to be a very informal space, the seating in the den (RIGHT) was slipcovered in durable, washable blue denim, which gets softer and paler with use. The coffee table is an antique Irish wake table with leaves. An American rag rug defines the seating area. Contemporary Southwestern rugs were used to make accessory pillows.

A guest bedroom in the addition designed by architect Lilian Rice in 1931 has brick floors and arched glass doors leading to a small back garden. The pine beds are Swedish and the coverlets are crocheted. The bedside table is a Mexican antique.

carefully detailed playhouse was built near the pool. According to an old newspaper clipping, the property was named Rancho del Oso (ranch of the bear) because a pet bear cub was kept lumbering around on the grounds.

After the Depression hit, the property was sold to a local couple, whose previous marriages had given them each a set of children. They needed extra space for their combined family and in 1931 hired Lilian Rice to design an addition for the house. Rice designed a two-bedroom and bath extension of the bedroom wing, blending it flawlessly with the existing smooth stucco walls and red-clay tile roof. Taking her cue from the previous architect, she opened the bedroom doors to the outside and extended the protective colonnade. During the couple's tenure at the house, the new bedroom wing was utilized to full capacity by the children, but the poolside playhouse was taken over for more adult activities. It became the locale of Friday night poker parties, and for many years, the open-house cardfests were a Rancho Santa Fe tradition.

By the time the Van Liews acquired the property, the house had acquired an alluring patina of age and the landscape had matured into a lush forest. Except for some kitchen remodeling, little had been done structurally to the house. After a few years, however, it became apparent to the Van Liews that things needed to be done to gently ease their 1920s treasure into the 1980s.

The bathrooms were updated and the floor plan reworked slightly in the bedroom wing so that short corridors now connect each of the bedrooms (just in case the weather is not quite so perfect). The remodeled bathrooms have tile and fixtures that are in keeping with the 1920s style. The master bath is lavished with handmade tile, and an airy feeling is created by a skylight and an adjacent private patio. The space was also slightly enlarged.

About the same time, Marcia Van Liew, with the help of Los Angeles interior designer Waldo Fernandez, tackled the main areas of the house. Extra lighting was installed in the living and dining rooms and den, hidden in the beams, and the furnishings were given a fresh look, suitable for family living.

In the living room, a cue was taken from the high ceilings and massive beams of the grand space, and overscale seating upholstered in simple fabrics was used to complement the setting. Other furnishings and accessories were chosen for their unfussy lines and scale as well. Many of the items, such as the Indian pottery, were acquired by the owners on their travels throughout the Southwest and Mexico.

The den is a casual place where everyone can relax without worrying about the condition of the furniture. The chairs, sofa, and double chaise are slipcovered in washable blue denim. And in the dining room, a long French refectory table, surrounded by antique Welsh Windsor chairs, sets the stage for more formal dinners.

Over the years the Van Liews have adapted to the wide-open, informal lifestyle that their hilltop house seems to command. They keep up with the citrus-growing hobby and have added a bountiful vegetable garden. The acreage came with equine privileges, so the acquisition of horses seemed natural.

Though subtly modernized, the Van Liews' house still conjures up images of Rancho Santa Fe's genteel past. It is a piece of history that allows its occupants to lead a very contemporary life.

The Van Liews had architect Edwin Hom enlarge their master bathroom (LEFT). The remodeled space was designed to have the creature comforts of today's new bathrooms yet blend harmoniously with the older architecture of the structure. The space was illuminated with a large skylight, cleverly disguised by a whitewashed grape-stake ceiling. The tile was handmade by Los Angeles artist Bette Chase. For the tub, chrome faucets were stripped down to the brass for a warmer look. The area rug is a contemporary Southwestern piece.

A private walled patio off the master suite (ABOVE) is favorite spot for reading on sunny winter days. The handmade hammock is from the Yucatán, the pillows from Oaxaca, Mexico. The tile mural is also from Mexico.

An old wooden yoke (TOP LEFT) found at an antiques shop in nearby Fallbrook has found a home on the exterior wall of the tool shed.

An ornate rack (BOTTOM LEFT) found in a local antiques shop holds old spurs, a lariat, and other decorative objects. The sleigh bells are used at Christmas—for musical accompaniment.

Two skulls (ABOVE) add ghostly, sculptural presence to an exterior wall. They were found in Baja California.

The back patio (RIGHT), which overlooks the pool, is the setting for informal Mexican food buffets. The fireplace, original to the house, is used often on cooler evenings. The doors lead into the living room.

DESERT MEDITERRANEAN

A SYNTHESIS OF
WARM-CLIMATE ARCHITECTURE
NORTH OF SAN DIEGO

The house (LEFT) was designed to take advantage of the region's temperate climate, as well as to be energy efficient. Deep overhangs not only provide shade for the terrace, but also protect the south- and west-facing windows from the intense summer sun. The L-shaped lap pool is seven feet deep at one end and has a whirlpool at the other. The pool's plaster was done in black for aesthetic reasons and because the dark color retains the heat of the sun longer than a conventionally colored pool.

Stairs (RIGHT) lead from the courtyard down to the garage and driveway. The overscale front door is bleached pine, stained platinum.

Northeast of the city of San Diego, the landscape undulates with gentle, grassy hills and broad sweeping valleys. The San Dieguito River cuts its path here, flowing westward toward the Pacific. Following the river's valley inland, the suburbs give way to a more rural setting; the countryside becomes hopscotched with fields of bright green strawberry plants and fenced, shady horse ranches. Here, on a knoll in the small town of Olivenhain, the contemporary new house of designers Ken Ronchetti and Linda Campbell rises majestically above the scene. At first glance, the soaring structure is definitively American and modern, but on closer study it becomes apparent that its design is a synthesis of cultures, time periods, and philosophies. Most important, the deceptively simple layout of the house allows the owners to lead a carefree lifestyle both indoors and out, taking full advantage of the region's temperate year-round climate.

The concept for the house took many years to develop; essentially, it is a distillation of ideas and techniques that Ken Ronchetti has used for other clients. "We've been working in

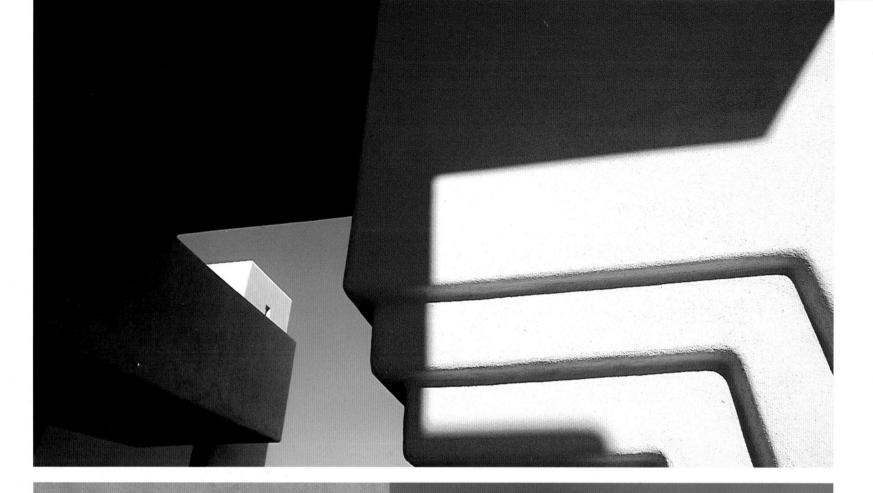

The influences of various architectural styles—both ancient and new—are evident in the house. The square was used as the basic design theme. Although the angular geometry is readily apparent on the exterior, the edges are slightly rounded, as if softened by time. The color for the exterior walls was selected by painting entire towers in different hues, then watching the effect of the sunlight. A pale amber color was finally chosen because it appeared rosy in the mornings, golden at dusk.

A small collection of seashells and coral from beaches around the world rests on the Texas shellstone coffee table (ABOVE).

this vein for several years now," he explains, "but this is by far the simplest manifestation of those ideas."

Before the Olivenhain home was built, the couple lived for some ten years in a tiny beach house in nearby Del Mar, while Ken Ronchetti built up his architectural practice, moving from commercial design into more and more residential commissions. Linda Campbell, in the meantime, ran the business end of the firm and did some landscape design as well.

Between projects, the couple became inveterate travelers, drawn to countries with warm climates, chasing the sun and, in essence, their favorite season—summer. While traveling, they noted and admired the local architecture: the mystery and spirit of Mayan temples in southern Mexico and Central America, the classic lines of old Roman villas, the whitewashed simplicity of Mediterranean houses. In Indonesia, they appreciated the coolness of the ubiquitous bungalows and their serene, hidden gardens; in Mexican coastal resorts, they enjoyed architecture in which it was difficult to determine where the interior ended and the outdoors began. In those countries, they discovered, they could also enjoy the simple indoor/outdoor lifestyle they sought in California.

For their planned house, they wanted to do more than just create a house inspired by warm-climate architecture. They wanted their house to be a sensitive structure, incorporating the design and energy philosophies of men they admired. The late inventor and designer R. Buckminster Fuller, with whom Ronchetti studied in the early 1960s, was an influ-

An eighteen-foot drop of mosquito netting keeps the terrace between the main room and the studio comfortable for outdoor relaxation. To keep the distinction between indoor and outdoor living delightfully vague, straw-colored Spanish tile decking was used both inside and out. The owners also avoided buying "patio furniture," instead moving their indoor pieces outside whenever the spirit or the weather inspires them.

ence, particularly because of his viewpoint that man should work with the forces of the universe rather than attempting to overcome them. Ronchetti also felt that Fuller's emphasis on synergism could be translated into architecture. They also admired futurist designer Paolo Soleri of Arizona for his work with passive solar designs that free structures from dependence on fossil fuels. Finally, they studied the work of Mexican architect Luis Barragan, who worked with simple lines and materials to create beautiful, romantic buildings. Barragan built homes that were protective, private, and always used water—a fountain, a pool—to cool warm-climate architecture.

After a decade of such architectural honing, the couple was ready to bring these experiences and ideas into fruition. They acquired a parcel of land on a hill and devised a straightforward plan: a three-room structure that opened onto a front courtyard, which could be used as an outdoor "room." Emphasis was placed on the use of natural ventilation and solar technology, allowing the house to be even more compatible with the forces of nature. The mostly sunny, moderate climate of southern California made it easy for the couple to think in terms of energy efficiency.

The 2,700-square-foot house is a pavilion-like building supported by lofty towers that draw the eye upward and give the house a sense of volume. Deep overhangs on the front of the house prevent the plan from seeming excessively vertical. Of a frame and plaster construction, the house employs the square as the basic design theme. The floor plan, for example, is two offset squares (the master bedroom and the studio) connected by a rectangle (the main room). Details, such as small gold-leaf squares set into the plastered walls inside the house, reiterate the theme.

Entry to the house from the driveway is through a bleached cedar-post gate and up a short flight of stairs,

From the exterior, the seating area of the main room is aglow in the evening (LEFT). Instead of a sofa, a comfortable arrangement of black leather chairs was used. The Texas shellstone coffee table was the designer's innovation; it is supported by four upturned terra-cotta pots. Behind are built-in bookshelves.

With the ten-foot-high glass walls pushed open, the terrace and the dining area become one large room (RIGHT). The overscale pine table was done by a local craftsman, Michael York. The chairs are wicker. The outdoor fireplace takes the chill off a cool evening.

The kitchen is centrally located in the main room, allowing the owners to converse with guests as they cook. Built-in lighting in the kitchen can be dimmed when dinner is served, thereby de-emphasizing the work area.

231

In the master suite (LEFT), which has its own heating and cooling system separate from the rest of the house, a free-standing wall separates the sleeping area from the bath. Closets on the left help to insulate the house from the fierce western sun. The clerestory windows, which can be opened, and the ceiling fan provide cross-ventilation.

In the bathroom (ABOVE), built-in shelves provide ample storage for linens and towels. Above the vanity, the mirrors are floated out from the wall and backlit, giving an illusion of depth. A window that opens and a venting skylight in the shower allow dampness to dissipate quickly. The white tile on the vanity and in the shower is from Guadalajara, Mexico.

whereupon the lush courtyard comes into view. With their desire to live outdoors as much as in, the couple lavished as much attention on planning the courtyard as they did the interior spaces. In this garden, Linda Campbell worked her wonders, along with the help of landscape designer Michael Bliss. They filled the space with deep yellow day lilies, palms, coral trees, and plumeria. A black-plastered lap pool (all that is needed for a cool soak and good exercise) turns left and connects with an outdoor whirlpool. One tower, supporting the front overhang, houses an outdoor fireplace, which is

Built-in bookshelves stretch along one wall of the main room. The curving stairs lead up to the master suite.

used regularly during the cooler winter months. Throughout the courtyard, they used straw-colored Spanish tile as the decking material, which was keyed into the pale amber color of the house's exterior walls.

The low, masonry courtyard wall and enclosed subtropical garden are more than just complements to the architecture, however. They provide protection from the area's inevitable summer brush fires; in the event of a fire, the water-filled garden area will serve as a buffer zone between the flames and the house itself.

Just outside the courtyard wall, the hillside has been revegetated with native plants. Eucalyptus, fountain grass, natal plum and lemonade berry, an evergreen shrub, as well as other low-water-use groundcovers, will eventually take over and make it seem as though there was never any construction on the hill.

Inside the house, the same tile was chosen for the flooring as in the courtyard, immediately establishing a connection between the two spaces. The main room of the house encompasses an open kitchen and dining and seating areas. In the seating section, another of the architectural towers holds a fireplace. Vast corner windows direct views to the scrub-covered hills beyond. Across from the windows, built-in book niches line a wall, and another tower conceals the powder room. The dining table is adjacent to the floor-to-ceiling sliding glass wall, which, when opened, offers unencumbered access to the courtyard, creating an extension of the main room.

At one end of the main room, curving steps lead up to the master suite, where closet space, floated in the middle of the room, divides the sleeping area from the bath. At the opposite end of the main room is Ken Ronchetti's at-home studio, which doubles as a guest room, complete with full bath. The studio also has sliding glass walls, opening it onto the courtyard.

The interior is decidedly contemporary, with the palette limited to black, white, and straw. The look is spare; furnishings are bold, simple. In the seating area, four overscale black leather chairs, used in lieu of a sofa, and a large Texas shellstone coffee table are enough to set the tone. The generous dining table and its grand rattan chairs move easily from inside out onto the courtyard. For the most part, the tile floors were kept bare of area rugs, and, except in the private areas, the windows were left uncovered. The impact of the interior comes from the architecture.

235

In the studio (LEFT), which also doubles as a guest room, an enormous Oriental fan is displayed over the futon. The futon, a Japanese-style cotton sleeping mat, folds up into a sofa by day.

A short curved hallway (RIGHT) connects the studio with the main room. Lighted niches are reminiscent of detailing found in the Pueblo-style architecture of New Mexico and Arizona. In the kitchen beyond, a venting skylight and a ceiling fan usher out warm air.

The house's lighting plan utilizes state-of-the-art technology. Though by day the house is naturally illuminated and has a resort-like ambience, by night it is dramatically lit, not unlike a big-city penthouse. After nightfall, the house takes on a romantic, even sexy atmosphere. Ceiling light fixtures are on touch-sensitive dimmers, allowing the exact mood to be set. The lights in the kitchen can be dimmed and those above the dining table brightened, thereby receding the work area.

Throughout the house, a sensitivity to energy efficiency is evident. The house is situated to have a southwestern exposure, capturing the warmth of the low winter sun and shielding the house from the higher summer sun with the overhangs. In the winter months, the sun's heat is absorbed by the tile flooring, making it comfortable to walk barefoot, and the mass of the fireplaces holds the heat as well. Along the northern and western walls of the house (the coldest and hottest sides), the structure was double-insulated with storage space. Bathroom cabinets, kitchen pantries, and clothing closets all snake their way around those sides of the house, buffering from heat and cold. Clerestory windows and glass walls provide excellent cross-ventilation. There are also venting skylights in each room, operable with the touch of a switch. Ceiling fans suspended from these skylights help heat escape during the summer. Their power reversed, the fans push warm air downward during the cooler seasons. Solar panels on the roof heat water. Even the pool, with its narrow surface area and deep color, holds the sun's heat longer than a conventional pool. Just outside the laundry room, in the back of the house, an area that receives direct, intense solar exposure was the spot to erect some very modern clotheslines, where damp beach towels dry in a few short hours.

Seemingly, all the careful planning has worked. The couple finds that life in the house is even better than they expected. Ronchetti frequently designs in the studio and holds client meetings in the courtyard, where gentle breezes and magnificent vistas do more for sparking a client's enthusiasm than a hundred renderings and sample books. They entertain often, hosting small dinners both inside and out. Outdoors, at night, margaritas are served, the fireplace is lit, and those who wish can relax in the whirlpool. Weekending guests often remark that the house is similar in feeling to resorts along the Mexican coast . . . or the Riviera, for that matter. "This house has a calming effect on us," notes Ken Ronchetti. "It is a resort we can live in every day."

Sweeping stretches of terrace, fascinating cloud formations, and steady breezes off the nearby Pacific are inducements to remain outside and enjoy the breathtaking vistas of the Southwest.

239

SOURCES

ACCESSORIES

DOODLET'S SHOP
120 Don Gaspar Avenue
Santa Fe, NM 87501
505-983-3771
Contemporary and antique New Mexican folk art, including tinwork; toys, books, and gifts.

DOS CABEZAS
6166 North Scottsdale Road
Scottsdale, AZ 85253
602-991-7004
Imported Mexican decorative objects, furniture, and fashions.

EL PASO SADDLE BLANKET COMPANY
5000 Alameda Avenue
El Paso, TX 79905
915-772-5267
Mexican saddles, wool saddle blankets, leather goods, and rugs.

THE HEARD MUSEUM SHOP
22 East Monte Vista Road
Phoenix, AZ 85004
602-252-8344
Fine Native American pottery, baskets, blankets, weaving, and jewelry.

LEE'S INDIAN CRAFTS
1833 East Indian School Road
Phoenix, AZ 85016
602-266-9432
Contemporary and antique Native American basketry and weaving.

LIPPER
5085 Westheimer
Houston, TX 77056
713-622-0705
Antique and new silver.

MAGGIE'S
3213 Knox
Dallas, TX 75205
214-520-3031
Dried flowers, herbs, antique linens, and other miscellany.

PENNYSMITH'S LTD.
4022 Rio Grande Boulevard NW
Albuquerque, NM 87107
505-345-2383
Folk art, antiques, and crafts.

QUÉ PASA
7051 East Fifth Avenue
Scottsdale, AZ 85251
602-990-7528
Contemporary Southwestern crafts and furniture; interior design service.

TARA TUCKER
137 East Palace
Santa Fe, NM 87501
505-983-6913
Antique and contemporary linens, antique quilts, and pine and cedar bedroom furniture.

THUNDERBIRD SHOP
40 West Broadway
Tucson, AZ 85701
602-623-1371
Native American art and crafts.

TOM BAHTI INDIAN ARTS
450 West Paseo Redondo
Tucson, AZ 85701
602-628-7029
Contemporary Native American crafts.

ANTIQUE AND CONTEMPORARY FURNITURE

BARROW'S FURNITURE
2301 East Camelback
Phoenix, AZ 85016
602-955-7550
Contemporary furniture; interior design service.

B. BROCK'S
2923 Henderson
Dallas, TX 75206
214-824-0671
Eclectic contemporary furniture and decorative objects.

BEYOND HORIZONS
7050 East Third Avenue
Scottsdale, AZ 85251
602-994-3359
Contemporary Southwestern furniture and crafts; interior design service.

CALDARELLA'S ANTIQUES
10167 Socorro Drive
El Paso, TX 79927
915-859-4777
Spanish Colonial and country pine furniture.

CORNER SHOP
360 Decorative Center
Dallas, TX 75207
214-741-1780
English country antiques.

DONDI
6024 Paseo Delicias
Rancho Santa Fe, CA 92067
619-944-9010

and

5100 Beltline Road, Suite 228
Dallas, TX 75240
214-392-9922
Antique and contemporary furniture and decorative objects.

E.C. DICKEN, INC.
1505-A Oak Lawn Avenue
Dallas, TX 75207
214-742-4801
American and European antiques; fine contemporary furniture.

HOLLER AND SAUNDERS, LTD.
PO Box 2151
Nogales, AZ 85628
602-287-4593
Importers of Mexican, South American, Asian, and European antiques and architectural components.

INSIDE
715 Eighth Avenue
San Diego, CA 92101
619-233-8201
Contemporary American and European furniture and lighting.

MODERN AGE
3013 East McDowell Road
Phoenix, AZ 85008
602-275-2711
Contemporary furniture and lighting; architect-designed classic furniture; interior design service.

REED BROTHERS
Turner Station
Sebastopol, CA 95472
707-795-6261
Manufacturers of hand-carved redwood and pine furniture.

ROCHE-BOBOIS
200 Madison Avenue
New York, NY 10016
Contemporary European furniture; store locations throughout the United States.

SANTA FE INTERIORS
214 Old Santa Fe Trail
Santa Fe, NM 87501
505-988-2227
Santa Fe-style willow furniture; Ponderosa pine beds.

SEMI POLITE FURNITURE
COMPANY
PO Box 97
Gallina, NM 87017
505-638-5606
Rough-hewn contemporary furniture with a sense of humor.

SOUTHWEST SPANISH
CRAFTSMAN
112 West San Francisco Street
Santa Fe, NM 87501
505-982-1767
Southwestern, Spanish Provincial, and Spanish Colonial handmade furniture and doors.

SUSAN SCHOEN'S ANTIQUES
218 Rue Chartres
New Orleans, LA 70130
504-522-3228
American and European antiques.

TAOS FURNITURE
232 Galisteo Street
Santa Fe, NM 87504
505-988-1229
Reproductions of New Mexican antique furniture.

TAOS STYLE FURNITURE
PO Box 858
Taos, NM 85751
505-758-8455
Taos-style handmade furniture.

JIM WAGNER, PAINTED
FURNITURE
PO Box 2110
Taos, NM 87571
505-758-8721
Contemporary hand-painted furniture.

ARCHITECTS, DESIGNERS, AND CONTRACTORS

MICHAEL BLISS & ASSOCIATES
221 Sunset
Encinitas, CA 92024
619-753-8261
Landscape design. Consultant for Ronchetti/Campbell house.

WILLIAM P. BRUDER, ARCHITECT
PO Box 4575 New River Stage
New River, AZ 85029
602-266-7399
Contemporary commercial and residential design services. Architect for Rosenbaum house.

BUTLER PRODUCTS
Mark Butler
Tucson, AZ 85749
602-749-2331
Residential and commercial construction. Builder/designer of own house.

COLONIAS BUILDERS, INC.
Mark Wilson
PO Box 2523
Taos, NM 87571
505-776-8185
General contractor for Troy house.

COOK CONSTRUCTION
James Cook
1308 North Fifth
Alpine, TX 79830
915-837-5780
Contractor for McIntyre-Morrow Ranch remodeling.

DESIGN & BUILDING
CONSULTANTS
Paul Weiner
40 East Fourteenth Street
Tucson, AZ 85701
602-792-0873
Custom architectural design and construction; also specializes in historical restorations. Consultant for Toci house.

EARTH AND SUN ADOBE
John Meechem
1246 East Inca
Mesa, AZ 85203
602-962-6751
Adobe home contractor.

ROSS STERLING EVANS
4905 Meadow Lark
El Paso, TX 79912
915-584-1755
Specializes in architect-designed houses. General contractor for McGregor house.

GARLAND & HILLES ARCHITECTS
David Hilles, AIA
1444 Montana
El Paso, TX 79902
915-533-3937
Contemporary commercial and residential design services. Architect for McGregor house.

EDWIN K. HOM, ARCHITECT
4407 Manchester Avenue, Suite 102
Encinitas, CA 92024
619-942-8080
Architect for Van Liew house remodeling.

ANTOINE PREDOCK, ARCHITECT
300 Twelfth Street NW
Albuquerque, NM 87102
505-843-7390
Contemporary, regionally inspired commercial and residential design services. Architect for Troy house.

WARREN RINGHEIM INTERIOR
DESIGN
Studio Antiques
320 Pine
Monroe, LA 71201
318-387-1051
*Antiques; interior design assistance
for Troy house.*

KEN RONCHETTI DESIGN, INC.
1302 Camino del Mar
Del Mar, CA 92014
619-481-0621
*Architectural, interior, and land-
scape design. Designer of own
house.*

STEWART CONSTRUCTION
COMPANY, INC.
Betty Stewart
503 Old Santa Fe Trail
Santa Fe, NM 87501
505-983-8797
*Adobe residential design and con-
struction. Designer/builder for Josey
house.*

WILLIAM TULL, ARTIST AND
DESIGNER
7610 East McDonald Drive
Scottsdale, AZ 85253
602-998-3151
*Specializing in contemporary adobe
houses. Designer of Pinnacle Peak,
Arizona house.*

WALDO'S DESIGNS
Waldo Fernandez
620 North Almont Drive
Los Angeles, CA 90069
213-659-6757
*Commercial and residential inte-
riors. Interior designer for Van Liew
house.*

ARCHITECTURAL MATERIALS AND REMNANTS

BARNETT AND DEYOE
701 West Silverlake Road
Tucson, AZ 85713
602-623-2662
Demolition yard.

DEL PISO
7816 Miramar Road
San Diego, CA 92126
619-566-9090
and
33 West Broadway
Mesa, AZ 85202
602-898-8989
Masonry, tile, and stone.

FACINGS OF AMERICA
4121 North Twenty-seventh Street
Phoenix, AZ 85016
602-955-9217
Imported and domestic tiles.

GARDEN STONE SUPPLY
2830 Grand Avenue
Phoenix, AZ 85017
602-262-9401
*Tile, marble, limestone, and
flagstone.*

GERSON'S DEMOLITION
1415 East Factory Avenue
Tucson, AZ 85719
602-624-8585
*Demolition yard; architectural
remnants.*

MEXICAN TILE COMPANY
2222 East Thomas Road
Phoenix, AZ 85016
602-954-6271
Custom tiles and murals.

OLD PUEBLO ADOBE COMPANY
5955 North El Camino del Terra
Tucson, AZ 85741
602-293-3206
Adobe, timbers, and vigas.

WESTLAKE ARCHITECTURAL
ANTIQUES
3315 West Westlake
Austin, TX 78746
512-327-1110
*Old fireplaces, transoms, stained
glass, and other architectural
remnants.*

WILSON INDUSTRIAL DOORS
Route 1, Box 47
Walworth, WI 53184
414-275-6869
Hangar door in McGregor house.

CRAFTSPEOPLE

BROTHER SUN, LTD.
2943 North Stone Avenue
Tucson, AZ 85705
602-622-1146
*Restoration and repair of adobe
houses.*

JOSEPH CANNIZZARO
1825 Kay Cee Lane
Prescott, AZ 86301
602-455-2735
Stonemason for Rosenbaum house.

FRANCISCO AND GARY CRUZ
231 West Ohio
Tucson, AZ 85701
602-628-6225 or 294-2141
*Stonemasons for Bernstein house
addition.*

GILBERT AND CHANG
16021 Arminta Street
Van Nuys, CA 91406
213-988-6710
Handmade tile.

CHRISTOPHER HEEDE
7007 East Rancho Del Oro Drive
Scottsdale, AZ 85255
602-488-2630
*Hand-thrown basins in Rosenbaum
house.*

LAURENT CONSTRUCTION
Ken Laurent and Mickey Laurent
8424 East Oak
Scottsdale, AZ 85257
602-946-6907
*Cabinetry and finish carpentry for
Rosenbaum house.*

GEORGE LOPEZ AND SABINITA
LOPEZ
Cordova, NM 87523
505-351-4572
*Carved santos in the finest New
Mexican tradition.*

MONTBLEAU & ASSOCIATES
335 West Sixth Street
San Diego, CA 92101
619-232-2859
Cabinetry for Ronchetti/Campbell house.

DAVID PLATT
APPLIED ARCHITECTURAL METALS
PO Box 961
Sedona, AZ 86336
602-282-1990
Metalwork for Rosenbaum house.

KAREN WILLIAMS
504 South Sixteenth Street
Alpine, TX 79830
915-837-5187
Stained glass artist for McIntyre-Morrow house.

YORK SPIRAL STAIR
North Vassalboro, ME 04962
207-872-5558
Hand-carved oak stair in McGregor house.

GALLERIES

DAVIS MATHER FOLK ART
GALLERY
141 Lincoln Avenue
Santa Fe, NM 87501
505-983-1600
New Mexican contemporary folk art.

ELAINE HORWITCH GALLERIES
4211 North Marshall Way

Scottsdale, AZ 85251
602-945-0791
and
129 West Palace
Santa Fe, NM 87501
505-988-8997
Also locations in Sedona, Arizona, and Palm Springs, California. Representing Bill Schenck and other Southwestern artists.

FENN GALLERIES LTD.
1075 Paseo de Peralta
Santa Fe, NM 87501
505-982-4631
Paintings by the old Santa Fe and Taos artists.

GALLERY 10
7045 Third Avenue
Scottsdale, AZ 85251
602-994-0405
and
225 Canyon Road
Santa Fe, NM 87501
505-983-9707
Representing Native American and contemporary Southwestern artists.

THE GALLERY WALL
104 Old Santa Fe Trail
Santa Fe, NM 87501
505-988-4168
and
7122 North Seventh Street

Phoenix, AZ 85020
602-943-8183
The work of Alan Houser, Dan Namingha, and others.

THE HAND AND THE SPIRIT
GALLERY
4222 North Marshall Way
Scottsdale, AZ 85251
602-949-1262
Fine contemporary crafts and jewelry.

MARILYN BUTLER FINE ART
4160 North Craftsman Court
Scottsdale, AZ 85251
602-994-9550
Representing Fritz Scholder and other Southwestern artists.

MICHAEL BERNSTEIN
Route 15, Box 274
Tucson, AZ 85715
602-299-5938
Specializing in primitive arts.

PUEBLO VISTA GALLERY II
2461 South San Diego Avenue
Suite 206
San Diego, CA 92110
619-297-6647
Specializing in Native American artwork.

STABLE ART CENTER
PO Box 198
Taos, NM 87571
505-758-2036
Contemporary Southwestern sculpture and paintings.

SUZANNE BROWN GALLERY
7156 Main Street
Scottsdale, AZ 85251
602-945-8475
Representing contemporary Southwestern artists.

W.S. DUTTON RARE THINGS
138 Sena Plaza
Santa Fe, NM 87501
505-982-5904
Native American historic pottery and baskets; New Mexican santos.

MUSEUMS

ALBUQUERQUE MUSEUM
2000 Mountain Road NW
PO Box 1293
Albuquerque, NM 87103
505-766-7878
Crafts, artifacts, and art of Albuquerque and New Mexico.

THE HEARD MUSEUM
22 East Monte Vista Road
Phoenix, AZ 85004
602-252-8848
The leading private museum of anthropology and primitive art in the Southwest.

MUSEUM OF INTERNATIONAL
FOLK ART
706 Camino Lejo
Santa Fe, NM 87504
505-827-8350
Folk art from the world over.

MUSEUM OF MAN
1350 El Prado
Balboa Park
San Diego, CA 92101
619-239-2001
Museum of culture and anthropology.

TEXAS MEMORIAL MUSEUM
2400 Trinity
Austin, TX 78705
512-471-1604
Emphasizing Native American and ranching history of Texas.

ORGANIZATIONS

ARIZONA HISTORICAL SOCIETY
949 East Second Street
Tucson, AZ 85701
602-628-5774
and
1242 North Central Avenue
Phoenix, AZ 85004
602-255-4479
Preservation of Arizona history, operation of two museums.

HISTORICAL SOCIETY OF NEW MEXICO
PO Box 5819
Santa Fe, NM 87502
505-983-6948
Preservation of the history of New Mexico.

LINCOLN COUNTY HERITAGE TRUST
Lincoln, NM 88338
505-653-4372
Dedicated to the preservation of Lincoln County's history.

PUBLICATIONS

ARCHITECTURAL DIGEST
5900 Wilshire Boulevard
Los Angeles, CA 90036
800-421-4448

ARIZONA HIGHWAYS MAGAZINE
2039 West Lewis Avenue
Phoenix, AZ 85009
602-258-6641

AUSTIN HOMES & GARDENS
900 West Avenue
Austin, TX 78701
512-479-8936

DALLAS–FORT WORTH HOME & GARDEN
2930 Turtle Creek Plaza, Suite 114
Dallas, TX 75219
214-522-1320

HISTORIC PRESERVATION
1785 Massachusetts Avenue, NW
Washington, DC 20036
202-673-4000

HOME
5900 Wilshire Boulevard
Los Angeles, CA 90036
213-938-3756

HOUSE & GARDEN
350 Madison Avenue
New York, NY 10017
212-880-8800

HOUSTON HOME & GARDEN
PO Box 25386
Houston, TX 77265
713-524-3000

JOURNAL OF ARIZONA HISTORY
Arizona Historical Society
949 East Second Street
Tucson, AZ 85701
602-628-5774

METROPOLITAN HOME
750 Third Avenue
New York, NY 10017
212-557-6600

NEW MEXICO MAGAZINE
1100 St. Francis Drive
Santa Fe, NM 87503
505-827-0220

PHOENIX HOME & GARDEN
3136 North Third Avenue
Phoenix, AZ 85013
602-234-0840

SAN DIEGO HOME & GARDEN
655 Fourth Avenue
San Diego, CA 92102
619-233-4567

SANTA FEAN
1440-A St. Francis Drive
Santa Fe, NM 87501
505-983-8914

SOUTHWEST ART MAGAZINE
PO Box 13037
Houston, TX 77219
713-850-0990

SUNSET MAGAZINE
80 Willow Road
Menlo Park, CA 94025
415-321-3600

TUCSON LIFESTYLE
7000 Tanque Verde Road, Suite 13
Tucson, AZ 85715
602-721-2929

TUCSON MAGAZINE
6720 Camino Principal, Suite 104
Tucson, AZ 85715
602-298-9455

BIBLIOGRAPHY

BOOKS

Alexander, Drury Blakely. *Texas Homes of the 19th Century.* Austin: University of Texas Press, 1966.

Armstrong, Ruth. *Enchanted Trails.* Santa Fe: New Mexico Magazine, 1980.

Beck, Warren A., and Haase, Ynez D. *Historical Atlas of New Mexico.* Norman: University of Oklahoma Press, 1985.

Boyd, E. *Popular Arts of Colonial New Mexico.* Santa Fe: Museum of International Folk Art, 1959.

Boyle, Bernard Michael. *Materials in the Architecture of Arizona, 1870–1920.* Tempe: Architecture Foundation of the College of Architecture, Arizona State University, 1976.

Bracken, Dorothy Kendall, and Redway, Maurine Whorton. *Early Texas Homes.* Dallas: Southern Methodist University Press, 1956.

Briggs, Charles. *The Woodcarvers of Cordova, New Mexico.* Knoxville: University of Tennessee Press, 1980.

Bunting, Bainbridge. *Of Earth and Timbers Made.* Albuquerque: University of New Mexico Press, 1974.

Casey, Robert L. *Journey to the High Southwest.* Seattle: Pacific Search Press, 1985.

Chauvenet, Beatrice. *Hewett and Friends.* Santa Fe: Museum of New Mexico Press, 1983.

Clotfelter, Connie. *Echoes of Rancho Santa Fe.* Rancho Santa Fe: CONREG, 1985.

Eldredge, Charles C., Schimmel, Julie, and Truettner, William H. *Art in New Mexico, 1900–1945.* New York: Abbeville Press, 1986.

Fehrenbach, T.R. *Lone Star.* New York: Macmillan Publishing Company, 1968.

Foster, Lynn V. *Spanish Trails in the Southwest.* New York: William Morrow & Company, 1986.

Gilbert, Fabiola Cabeza de Baca. *New Mexican Traditions and Food.* Santa Fe: Museum of New Mexico Press, 1982.

Grattan, Virginia L. *Mary Colter: Builder Upon the Red Earth.* Flagstaff, AZ: Northland Press, 1980.

Gray, Virginia, and Macrae, Alan. *Mud, Space and Spirit.* Santa Barbara, CA: Capra Press, 1976.

Harte, John Bret. *Tucson: Portrait of a Desert Pueblo.* Woodland Hills, CA: Windsor Publications, 1980.

Heimann, Jim, and Georges, Ripp. *California Crazy: Roadside Vernacular Architecture.* San Francisco: Chronicle Books, 1980.

Iowa, Jerome. *Ageless Adobe.* Santa Fe: Sunstone Press, 1985.

Jenkinson, Michael. *Land of Clear Light.* New York: E.P. Dutton & Company, 1977.

Kirker, Harold. *California's Architectural Frontier.* Santa Barbara, CA: Peregrine Smith, 1973.

Luckingham, Bradford. *The Urban Southwest: A Profile History of Albuquerque, El Paso, Phoenix and Tucson.* El Paso: Texas Western Press, 1982.

Luhan, Mable Dodge. *Winter in Taos.* Taos, NM: Las Palomas de Taos, 1982.

Lummis, Charles F. *Land of Poco Tiempo.* Albuquerque: University of New Mexico Press, 1928.

Maestas, José Griego, and Anaya, Rudolfo. *Cuentos: Tales from the Hispanic Southwest.* Santa Fe: Museum of New Mexico Press, 1980.

McAlester, Virginia, and Lee. *A Field Guide to American Houses.* New York: Alfred A. Knopf, 1984.

McCoy, Esther. *Five California Architects.* New York: Praeger Publishers, 1975.

McKeever, Michael. *A Short History of San Diego.* San Francisco: Lexicos, 1985.

McLuhan, T.C. *Dream Tracks.* New York: Harry N. Abrams, 1985.

Metz, Leon Claire. *City at The Pass: An Illustrated History of El Paso.* Woodland Hills, CA: Windsor Publications, 1980.

Miller, Tom. *Arizona: The Land and The People.* Tucson: University of Arizona Press, 1986.

Moorhead, Max L. *New Mexico Royal Road.* Norman: University of Oklahoma Press, 1958.

Nichols, John. *On the Mesa.* Salt Lake City: Peregrine Smith Books, 1986.

Shalkop, Robert L. *The Folk Art of a New Mexico Village.* Colorado Springs: Taylor Museum of the Colorado Springs Fine Arts Center, 1969.

Spears, Beverly. *American Adobes.* Albuquerque: University of New Mexico Press, 1986.

Speck, Lawrence, W. *Landmarks of Texas Architecture.* Austin: University of Texas Press, 1986.

Spellenberg, Richard. *The Audubon Society Field Guide to North American Wildflowers, Western Region.* New York: Alfred A. Knopf, 1979.

Steele, Thomas J. *Santos and Saints.* Albuquerque: Calvin Horn, 1974.

Sunset Books. *The California Missions.* Menlo Park, CA: Lane Book Company, 1964.

Taylor, Lonn, and Bokides, Dessa. *Carpenters and Cabinetmakers: Furniture Making in New Mexico, 1600–1900.* Santa Fe: Museum of New Mexico Press, 1983.

Tolbert, Frank X. *An Informal History of Texas.* New York: Harper & Brothers, Publishers, 1961.

Twitchell, Ralph Emerson. *Old Santa Fe Trail.* Santa Fe: Santa Fe New Mexican Publishing, 1925.

Williamson, Joseph F. *Sunset New Western Garden Book.* Menlo Park, CA: Lane Publishing Company, 1979.

Wissler, Clark. *Indians of the United States.* Garden City, NY: Doubleday & Company, 1966.

Writer's Program. *New Mexico: A Guide to the Colorful State.* New York: Hastings House, 1953.

Wroth, William. *Hispanic Crafts of the Southwest.* Colorado Springs: Taylor Museum, 1977.

PERIODICALS

Bassett, Carol Ann. "Roots of Regionalism: 'Great Stone Cities.'" *Architecture* (Washington, DC), March 1984, pp. 98–100.

———. "Roots of Regionalism: The Missions." *Architecture* (Washington, DC), March 1984, pp. 102–105.

Beard, Betty. "Barrio Libre Gains New Life in Long, Turbulent History." *Arizona Daily Star* (Tucson, AZ), January 11, 1972.

Cheek, Lawrence W. "Arizona's Architecture." *Arizona Highways Magazine* (Phoenix, AZ), May 1984, pp. 4–22.

"A Christmas Visit to Old Mesilla." *New Mexico Magazine* (Santa Fe, NM), December 1985, pp. 34–37.

Engelbrecht, Lloyd and June. "Prairie School Architect: Henry C. Trost." *Texas Homes* (Dallas, TX), November/December 1978, pp. 26–30.

Engelbrecht, Lloyd C. "The Prairie School in the Southwest." *The Prairie School Review* (Palos Park, IL), Fourth Quarter 1969, pp. 5–30.

Henn, Nora. "Lincoln County: A Historical Overview." *Rio Grande History* (Las Cruces, NM), Number 9, 1978, pp. 2–5.

Juliber, Lina. "Pinnacle Peak Village." *Phoenix Magazine* (Phoenix, AZ), February 1977, pp. 54–56.

Kanner, Diane. "May, The Master." *San Diego Home/Garden* (San Diego, CA), April 1986, pp. 34–39.

Kilcrease, Della. "Home: A History Lesson." *Las Cruces Sun-News* (Las Cruces, NM), April 10, 1983.

Liefgreen, Dan. "Residents and City Pleased with Annexation." *Scottsdale Daily Progress* (Scottsdale, AZ), January 5, 1983.

Michaelis, Dee. "3,100 Acre Project at Pinnacle Peak Approved." *Arizona Republic* (Phoenix, AZ), March 19, 1986.

Mittelbach, Margaret. "Dreamtracks." *Southwest Spirit Magazine* (Los Angeles, CA), May 1986, pp. 58–62.

Neary, Joan. "One Man's Fight to Save the Barrio." *Americana* (New York, NY), January-February 1979, pp. 45–48.

Olten, Carol. "Lilian Rice Set Rancho Santa Fe's Architectural Style." *The San Diego Union* (San Diego, CA), March 2, 1986.

Rotstein, Arthur H. "Mysteries of Mud." *Historic Preservation* (Washington, DC), February 1986, pp. 64–69.

Shipsky, James. "Six from the Sixties." *Architecture* (Washington, DC), January 1984, pp. 80–86.

Simpson, Babs. "A Passion for Purity." *House & Garden* (New York, NY), November 1983, pp. 164–169.

Stewart, Janet Ann. "Mansions of Main Street." *Journal Of Arizona History* (Tucson, AZ), Volume 20, Number 2, Summer 1979, pp. 193–222.

Sutro, Dirk. "The Far Pavilions." *San Diego Home/Garden* (San Diego, CA), November 1985, pp. 36–43.